What Others Are Saying

"Here's a book I wish I'd read when I was single and then single again after a divorce. Allison K. Flexer gets right to the heart of the problem many unmarried women face—believing lies about themselves that can only be overcome with the truths from God's Word."

—Karen O'Connor, author
In Step with Your Stepchildren,
The Beauty of Aging,
Gettin' Old Ain't for Wimps

"It's difficult to be single in a married persons' world. Allison K. Flexer validates the familiar feelings with which many single women struggle while bringing truth and light to the conversation. This book liberates single women from the lies that sound like truth."

—Kristi Marshall, PhD
Licensed Professional Counselor

"In her new book *Truth, Lies, and the Single Woman,* Allison K. Flexer shares the lessons that encouraged, comforted, and challenged her to overcome lies and seek her One True Love. Through the study of God's Word, Allison knows and teaches the truth."

—Vonda Skelton, author
Seeing Through the Lies

"Beautifully written with warmth and transparency, this important book effectively dispels the lies that often blindside single women. Allison K. Flexer seamlessly blends her tender stories with fresh insights from timeless biblical accounts. You may laugh, you may cry, but I guarantee you will highly benefit from the wisdom of one who has been there."

—Judy Gordon Morrow, author
The Listening Heart

Truth, Lies,
AND THE
Single
Woman

DISPELLING 10
COMMON MYTHS

BY
ALLISON K. FLEXER

BEACON HILL PRESS
OF KANSAS CITY

Beacon Hill Press of Kansas City
PO Box 419527
Kansas City, MO 64141
www.BeaconHillBooks.com

ISBN 978-0-8341-3363-1

Printed in the
United States of America

Cover Design: Claire Cork
Interior Design: Sharon Page

Library of Congress Cataloging-in-Publication Data

Flexer, Allison K.
    Truth, lies, and the single woman : dispelling 10 common myths / Allison K. Flexer.
        pages cm
    Includes bibliographical references.
    ISBN 978-0-8341-3363-1 (pbk.)
    1. Self-esteem in women—Religious aspects—Christianity. 2. Christian women—Reli-
gious life. 3. Single women—Religious life. I. Title.
    BV4527.F5947 2014
    248.8'432—dc23

                                                                    2014018992

10 9 8 7 6 5 4 3 2 1

For Lynn Husband
Thank you for guiding me on a journey of healing.
Your counsel made it possible for me to write these words.

Contents

Acknowledgments

Many people believed in this project and walked through years of highs and lows with me as this book took shape. Each of you is a part of this finished product.

First and foremost, I give the credit and gratitude to God. Lord, you are the only true Author. My words can never be adequate enough to describe how holy and loving you are.

Thank you to the single and married women and men who bravely took my surveys and allowed me to interview them. Your stories and quotes added so much depth to this book.

Michael: You are the answer to years and years of prayers. The long wait was worth it, and I'm very glad I didn't settle! I love you, and I'm grateful for you. Thank you for loving me so well and encouraging me to finish this project.

Mom, Dad, Susan, Luke, Maria, and Nadia: You inspire me and make me laugh until I cry. I love "us."

My friends, who give me a support net I can't live without and encourage me to be the best version of me: Chasie, Bess, Allison (A1), Amy, Susanna, Tanya, Zana, DeeDee, Hilary, Elizabeth, Susan, Jinanne, Lorrie, and Marye.

My Bible study girls (BSGs): Kristi, Suzette, Elizabeth, Robin, and Amy. Your prayers carried me through.

Tim and Karen White, James and Liz Wessel: Thank you for believing in me from the beginning, being role models for me, and letting me share your stories.

Judy Gordon Morrow, Karen O'Connor, Vonda Skelton, Edie Melson, Mary Hampton, and Lisa Bogart: A special thanks to each of you, my writing friends and mentors.

Carter Crenshaw: I am grateful for your teachings over the years. You shaped my understanding of grace and faith.

Stephanie and the Sisters at Sacred Heart Monastery in Cullman, Alabama: Thank you for allowing me to write at your beautiful retreat center. Your prayers provided much peace during this process.

Gabriele Udell and the team at Beacon Hill Press: You turned my dreams into reality. I am so grateful to you for believing in this project.

Rachel Kent, my agent: Thank you for guiding me through this process, giving me wise advice, and being a friend along the way.

Finally, to the directors, staff, and faculty at the Mount Hermon Christian Writers Conference: When I first set foot on campus five years ago, I *thought* I was a good writer. Thanks for breaking me down and building me back up with the skills and education I needed to become a published author.

Author's Note

All of the vignettes shared in *Truth, Lies, and the Single Woman* are true stories, including the author's own personal experiences shared in each chapter. None of the book is fictional. The women whose stories appear in the book were interviewed by the author or completed a survey developed by the author. However, many of the names have been changed to protect the identity of these women.

Introduction

Dear friend,

We are in a battle. Our enemy wants us to believe his lies instead of God's truth. Jesus called the devil a liar and the father of lies (John 8:44).

It is tempting for us—as single women—to believe we are not valuable. We believe we aren't worthy to be chosen. We become convinced we aren't beautiful or cherished. We think God has forgotten about us. Since we remain unmarried, we struggle with the lie that something must be wrong with us.

We can become so preoccupied with our single status that we're useless for God's kingdom. Through deception, Eve believed the lie that God wanted to keep something good from her. Do we think we're not susceptible to lies today?

> Stand firm then, with the belt of truth buckled around your waist.
> (Ephesians 6:14a)

Our enemy wants you to live a defeated life, never understanding the fullness of God's mighty love for you. Will you let him win? Or will you replace the lies with God's truth?

Finally, be strong in the Lord and in his mighty power. Put on the full armor of God, so that you can take your stand against the devil's schemes. For our struggle is not against flesh and blood, but against the rulers, against the authorities, against the powers of this dark world and against the spiritual forces of evil in the heavenly realms. (Ephesians 6:10-12)

Lie #1: Because no one has chosen me, I'm not valuable.

*S*weat rolled down my back as I stood against the hot, red brick wall. The sun blazed down on the small field. My classmates and I formed a line along the exterior wall of the elementary school gym. Squinting against the bright sun, I endured my least favorite part of the day. Why couldn't I be athletic like the other kids? The team captains began calling out names in an alternating rhythm: *Matt, Jennifer, Rob, Susie.* Fidgeting, I plastered a fake smile on my face while I waited. I made eye contact and silently begged the team captain to choose me next. Giving up, I stared down at my shoes. I knew the outcome before looking up. I was the last one against the wall. Again.

Back then, I excelled in the classroom and enjoyed all other aspects of school. However, when the hour came for gym class, I developed a case of what my sister and I deem "nervous stomach." That sick feeling of dread materialized deep in my gut when I lined up with my classmates as team captains chose their teams. As a skinny, uncoordinated girl who couldn't throw, kick, or dodge a ball, I dreaded being chosen last. Even next to last would ruin my day.

The nervous stomach feeling is a familiar one. It still sneaks up on me. I'm a thirty-six-year-old single woman. No one has chosen me. I'm still standing here against the brick wall—fidgeting, staring at my shoes, and hoping my name will be called next. Satan whispers a little lie, "You aren't worthy to be chosen. You weren't then and you aren't now."

Throughout my twenties, compatible mates chose each of my friends one by one. Now, in my thirties, the baby boom is here. Through it all, I continue to go on dates. It seems so childish compared to the big life changes my friends get to experience. Dating is now tiresome. My friends don't have to date anymore. I do. They have someone to kiss goodnight. I don't. At the end of a long day, they know who is going to be there.

They must be more worthy than me. What do they have that I don't? Is there some big secret I missed? Maybe a secret only shared with the kids who *weren't* chosen last in gym class?

> No person gives us our value, not even our beloved spouse. In fact, when you're married, you often have the magnifying glass on high and recognize your flaws and sins in an even greater way! God alone and our righteousness in Christ is all we can boast in.
>
> —Renee, 31, married

Do you feel this way? Do you struggle with allowing a relationship—or lack thereof—to determine your value? I tend to let external circumstances determine my value instead of turning to the only one who is able to make me feel complete: Jesus.

Jill's Story

My married friend Jill has the benefit of looking back on her single years with some perspective. As I sat on the window seat in her bright kitchen, she cooked dinner for her family and reminisced about those years. "When I was single, I always looked at marriage and motherhood as the Promised Land," she recalled. "I believed once I got there, everything would be perfect."

As I processed Jill's comment, her three-year-old daughter ran into the room, crying because her little sister hurt her arm and accidentally knocked the bowl of flour out of her mom's hands. Flour-covered Jill turned to me and declared, "Well, obviously everything still isn't perfect. We're always dealing with one thing or the other."

She wisely noted how marriage isn't the solution for a perfect life. Jill admitted to me that she often gets distracted from God because of her duties as a wife and mother. She recalled her single years honestly. "I don't think I was ever thankful for my single years and the good time I had with the Lord," she said.

Jill's outlook caught me off guard. My friend's words made me realize I have ample time and opportunity to put God first now, but someday that may not always be the case. My friend's parting advice that day still echoes in my head. "If you can move toward God and work on putting your identity in him as a single girl, you'll have such an easier time in marriage and motherhood."

Why is it hard for us to depend on God for our value? It's obviously the right answer. For me, it becomes difficult when I'm lonely. Is he going to snuggle on the couch with me and watch a movie? Not in my experience. On those lonely days, I struggle to remember that my relationship with him is enough. Especially when years have passed and my desires are still here, but unmet.

I may never get married. I may never have children. Ouch. Those statements are painful because I truly desire to be married and have children. I avoid saying those words aloud because it makes me feel less validated, less worthy, and less of a person.

As single women, we often feel overlooked. We start believing the lies and asking difficult questions. Who am I if no one loves me? What if no one chooses to spend his life with me?

Truth: You are chosen by the one who matters most—God.

God chose you to be his daughter. In Isaiah 41:9b-10, God says, "I have chosen you and have not rejected you. So do not fear, for I am with you; do not be dismayed, for I am your God. I will strengthen you and help you; I will uphold you with my righteous right hand."

Nothing surprises God. Since you belong to God, he knows exactly who you are and where you are. He understands when you feel lonely and when you feel left behind. He works all things together for good.

His ways are higher than my ways. When I start doubting my worth—when I start feeling like the kid in gym class who was chosen last—I read these excerpts from Psalm 139 and substitute my name for each personal pronoun in the passage:

You have searched *me*, LORD, and you know *me*. . . .
You perceive *my* thoughts from afar. . . .
You are familiar with all *my* ways. . . .
You lay your hand upon *me*. . . .
(Psalm 139:1-3, 5, emphasis mine)

Isn't that what we all truly desire? We want to be known completely and loved unconditionally. God fills that void in us. Actually, he is the *only* one who can fill it permanently. All other sources are substitutes, and they will fade with time.

Now that we know we're chosen by God and precious to him, what does that really mean? Most importantly, he desires for us to choose him back. He longs for us to seek a relationship with him as our first priority: "But seek first his kingdom and his righteousness, and all these things will be given to you as well" (Matthew 6:33).

In *My Utmost for His Highest*, Oswald Chambers writes, "Jesus is saying that the great care of the life is to put the relationship to God first, and everything else second." Chambers points out we often argue, "But I must live; I must make so much money; I must be clothed; I must be fed."[1]

I understand these arguments. It's easy to let the physical concerns of this world take first place in our hearts. We get caught up living on this earth and not living for eternity. The things that matter in this world will matter little in the next. Yet we focus so much of our energy on making ourselves comfortable and attaining things in this world. What if we redirected that energy into our relationship with God?

It's easy for me to shift God into second place. The things I most desire may be godly things—marriage, children, and family. Nothing is wrong with those desires. However, when I let those desires become primary, I shift God right out of first place.

I fall for the lie that tangible relationships here on earth will fill the void in my soul. They won't. I hope a husband will make me feel complete. He won't. God created us to crave relationship with him. No earthly relationship will be able to fill that part of us. We must look to him first and put everything else second.

To embrace our standing as daughters of God and believe that he is enough, we must first look at his character. "Who am I?" is a question best answered by asking, "Who is God?" The nature of God must be considered whenever Satan presents lies to us. In my life, the tough questions about loneliness and unmet desires are only fully answered when I understand the roles of God in my life.

God as Companion

Recently, I attended a conference for writers and speakers. The organizers set up a prayer room for attendees. The room highlighted the various names of God. As I entered the room for the first time, the mood of the darkened space quickly took over. Listening to the soft worship music play, I noticed pillows strategically placed on the floor and armchairs waiting to be claimed. Despite the number of women in the room, I heard no voices other than whispered prayers.

Curious about the names of God, I moved toward the tables at the end of the room. There were hundreds of personalized slips of paper, each printed with the name of a conference attendee, each one attached to a larger piece of paper that proclaimed a name of God from the Old Testament. I scanned hundreds of names looking for my own, hopeful that the conference team prayerfully linked up my name to just the right one.

I stopped and held my breath as I read:

Jehovah Shammah

The Lord Is There

The Lord My Companion

Even though I didn't realize it, my heart had been searching for this answer. I poured out my heart to God and confessed my loneliness. I admitted that even with all the great friends he provided me—even in the midst of six hundred amazing Christian women at the conference—I still wanted a companion. And the companion I wanted was a husband.

I think of God as my Rock, my Father, my Hiding Place, my Provider, and many other wonderful things. But God as my Companion? I never considered him in that role. But he knows exactly what I need at each moment.

A Scripture verse was noted on the paper:

"God is within her, she will not fall;

God will help her at break of day" (Psalm 46:5).

God knows and understands my needs deeply. He wants me to understand he is the only companion who will never fail. He is the one who is there—already within me—and the one who will love me without ceasing.

Even though he may not snuggle with me on the couch, God is the companion I'm truly seeking. All other solutions will fail to fill the void in my heart. Only God can satisfy my deep need to be known and loved. He created me with a longing for him, and seeking satisfaction or significance anywhere else is futile.

But what about the unmet desires that linger in my soul? I still want to get married and have a family. And honestly, on some days the thought of God as a loving companion just isn't enough.

God put these desires in my heart, but he asks me to surrender my plans and my timing to him. I like to believe I'm in control of my own life. I go around making plans and deciding how things will turn out. Unfortunately, control is only an illusion. As Donald Miller says, "This whole following Jesus business is largely about giving him control, or more, realizing we don't have control to begin with."[2]

When our plans and timetables don't work, we shake our fists at God. Instead of submitting to him, we hold on to our plans. We must put our desires second to our standing with Jesus. We must learn to surrender to God.

God as Provider

One of the most beautiful—yet difficult—pictures of surrender in the Bible is a story about Abraham and his son Isaac. Abraham waited a long time for a son. In the process of waiting, he learned to trust God. After years of waiting and praying, he finally held the fruit of God's promises—his son Isaac. It's a beautiful example of God answering prayer. But the story doesn't end with the birth of Isaac. In Genesis 22, God asked Abraham to give up his little boy. God told Abraham to sacrifice his only son as a burnt offering.

Can you imagine waiting all those years for your deep desire to be met? Once God answers your prayer, he immediately asks you to give up what he just gave you. By asking Abraham to give up Isaac, God was inquiring, "Do you trust me?"

When Abraham's son noticed they were headed to the mountain without an animal to sacrifice, he asked his father a difficult question. "Where is the lamb for the burnt offering?" (Genesis 22:7b). Abraham answered his little boy—no doubt tormented by what God requested—by saying, "God himself will provide" (v. 8). Abraham was confident God's plan was best, even though he didn't understand it. He didn't want to give up his son, but he trusted God to be his great and only provider.

What is the Isaac in your life? In my life, it's the desire to be married and have children. I am holding it tightly. God asks me to surrender my plans and timetables, placing them on the altar. He wants me to let go and turn it over to him. I want to be like Abraham. When God asks me to sacrifice my plans in exchange for him, I want to trust that he will provide. He always keeps his promises.

> Isaiah 30:15 has been my rock: "In repentance and rest is your salvation, in quietness and trust is your strength." You don't have to be your own source or rock holding it all together and forging the way. You can sit still, be quiet with God, and trust God. Give yourself a break. Slow down and breathe. Smile. God will give you strength!
>
> —Alexis, 29, single

I know God is big enough to forgive all my sins. I trust him with my eternal salvation. I believe God accepts me with open arms and extends his grace and mercy to me again and again. But sometimes, I still have trouble letting go and trusting him with the details. Trust him with my eternity? Sure. Trust him with tomorrow? Not so fast.

But trust is exactly what God asked Abraham to do. Even though Abraham doubted God in the past and made some big mistakes (which we'll see in the next chapter), God gave him this opportunity to trust. Admitting I have questions is not wrong—it's honest. We can be honest with God. But when we ask God difficult questions, we should also know his response will probably be, "Do you trust me?"

My first priority is not always the same as God's first priority. I imagine God's main concern is for me to become more like him—

not for me to get married before age thirty-five and have children before time runs out. Surrendering means giving up my priorities and asking God to align my plans with his divine priorities.

Like Abraham, I don't get it right every time. It's a journey of faith and a daily battle. Here is the prayer I often pray:

Lord, make my priorities match your priorities. Change my heart so that I desire what you desire. You know my needs better than I do. Meet my needs according to your will. Teach me to trust you more each day. Amen.

God as Hope

While in a hopeless place a few years ago, I started a journal of blessings on my computer. Each day, I typed one thing for which I was grateful. Even though I felt miserable and the days seemed dark, I forced myself to find one blessing in each day. I knew I needed to praise God, especially because I couldn't feel any hope.

The book of Proverbs declares truth in 13:12: "Hope deferred makes the heart sick." I have experienced the truth of this verse firsthand. After strug-

> The Lord is good to those whose hope is in him, to the one who seeks him; it is good to wait quietly for the salvation of the Lord.
>
> (Lamentations 3:25-26)

gling with the true meaning of this verse, I came to a new realization. What is hope? The definition of hope is Jesus. God sent Jesus as our only hope (see 1 Peter 1:3, 13; Titus 2:13; and 1 Timothy 1:1). When I defer Jesus in favor of circumstances, temporary happiness, or my own dreams, it makes my heart sick. When I put God in second place, it makes my heart sick. God designed us with a longing that can only be met by him. He wants to be our true Companion and Provider. Nothing else we use to fill that void will work.

When the lies start their daily march through my mind and when I believe I'm not worthy to be chosen, I immediately pause and remember the character of God. He is my Companion. He is my Provider. He is my Hope. I am chosen by him.

Remember those tough questions I raised earlier? "Who am I if no one loves me? What if no one chooses to spend his life with me?"

The truth is clear. I am a child of the King, the one who makes no mistakes, the one who created me in his image. Standing alone with nothing to offer, I am enough for him. I must surrender. I must cling to Jesus—my true source of hope.

● ● ●

I say to myself, "The LORD is my portion;
therefore I will wait for him."
(Lamentations 3:24)

Because no one has chosen me, I'm not valuable.

Women who believe this lie often say:

- No one has chosen me.
- Once I get married, everything will be okay.
- After someone chooses me, I will be complete.
- When I'm married, I will finally feel loved and valuable.
- Getting married will cure my loneliness.

You are chosen by the one who matters most—God.

God says:

- **I choose you.**
  For we know, brothers and sisters loved by God, that he has chosen you. (1 Thessalonians 1:4)
- **I am your Companion.**
  God is our refuge and strength, an ever-present help in trouble. (Psalm 46:1)
- **I am your Provider.**
  So Abraham called that place The LORD Will Provide. And to this day it is said, "On the mountain of the LORD it will be provided." (Genesis 22:14)
- **I am your Hope.**
  Yes, my soul, find rest in God; my hope comes from him. (Psalm 62:5)
- **I always keep my promises.**
  For he remembered his holy promise given to his servant Abraham. He brought out his people with rejoicing, his chosen ones with shouts of joy. (Psalm 105:42-43)

Lies I Believe:

....

....

....

....

....

....

....

....

....

Truth I Want to Remember:

....

....

....

....

....

....

....

....

....

Lie #2: *God has forgotten about me.*

When I was twenty-four years old, I found him—the love of my life and the man I intended to marry. Or so I thought. We planned to get engaged as soon as he came back from his latest deployment. He was a handsome army lieutenant. Thrilled to be part of a beautiful love story, I endured the six months of separation. Although it was difficult, I knew it would only make our love stronger. That is, until I found out about the other girl he was pursuing online.

Lying in my bed, I squeezed my eyes shut and reminded myself to breathe. I whined to God and pleaded for answers. *Why did this happen?* It truly had to be a big, cosmic mistake. Was God paying attention to some natural disaster while he allowed my life to slip through the cracks? How could my boyfriend abandon me? How could God forget about me? What did I do wrong to deserve this heartbreak? The unanswered questions plagued my mind and felt like lead weights settling in my stomach.

Somehow, I continued to get out of bed every day. Each morning, I woke up feeling peaceful and happy. And then, like a punch in the gut, I remembered everything. As the memories surfaced, I made my daily trip to the bathroom to be sick. Recalling how the love of my life chose someone else, I concluded that God abandoned me also.

When things don't go according to my plans, I assume God has forgotten about me. It's difficult for me to wait on the Lord at these times. In my heart, I know I can trust God with my future. In my head, I beg him to hurry up and move things along. As if he—the Creator of the universe and the One sovereign over all things—has somehow overlooked me.

Abandonment and rejection create fertile ground for our enemy to plant his lie. Many of us already believe we don't have value. In the wake of rejection, we accept the lie that God has forgotten about us. He's just too busy. With everything else going on in the world, why would he pay attention to my day-to-day circumstances? Sometimes we believe God doesn't care about our happiness.

Catherine's Story

My friend Catherine understands how rejection can lead us to have doubts about God's compassion. Catherine was single until the age of thirty-nine. Over the daily lunch special at a cute Italian bistro, she told me how she waited on God for years. And how she believed he had forgotten about her. I nodded and cringed knowingly when she recalled her prayer. "Lord, don't bring another man into my life unless he is the one I'm going to marry." I had recently prayed a very similar prayer. Catherine also quipped, "I always wonder if God laughs when we try to tell him what to do."

After making her petition known to God, Catherine met a great guy at church. They connected immediately and dated for about six months. She assumed it was finally her turn to find love. At this point, I thought Catherine would wrap up the story by saying, "And that's how I met my husband." Wrong. A new girl moved into town, and Catherine's beau decided that she was a better fit for him. He married the new girl, and they now have two children.

Catherine admitted to me that the rejection and disappointment caused her to sink into a depression. Having been through some dark times myself, I completely understood the despair she described. When you've been waiting for such a long time and allow yourself to experience a glimmer of hope, the letdown can be very rough. Catherine ended up meeting her husband somewhere she never expected while she wasn't looking—at work. Of course, she could trust God all along. As with any couple, there have been challenges in their relationship, but they are passionate about serving the Lord together.

Thinking back to the hopelessness she felt when she believed the lie that God had forgotten about her, Catherine recalled going through the book of Psalms and underlining every promise about how God hears her and hasn't forgotten about her. It reminded her that God cares about the desires of her heart, and she clung to his promises as she continued to wait. As we left the restaurant, she turned to me and said, "If you do marry, remember that your spouse cannot meet all of your needs. If he could, he would be God. Always remember *whose* you are."

Sarah's Story

In the Bible, we meet a woman who also thought God forgot about her. Sarah was married to Abraham. Sarah struggled in her marriage because she couldn't have children. She was impatient, and she didn't entrust the timing of such events to God. Instead, she decided to take matters into her own hands. She approached her husband and said, "The LORD has kept me from having children. Go, sleep with my slave; perhaps I can build a family through her" (Genesis 16:2). I don't know if Abraham was baffled or pleased, but he agreed to his wife's wild plan.

Sarah was tired of waiting, so she took control of the situation. God had already promised Abraham his offspring would be numerous (see Genesis 15:5). Sarah knew about the promise, but in her opinion, the plan wasn't being fulfilled quickly enough. She lowered her standards to hurry God's plans along.

How many times have I done this exact thing in my life? I desire to be married. I pray for God to bring the man into my life he wants me to marry. And then, I wait and wait some more. Probably just like you, I'm not sitting on my hands expecting God to drop my future husband in my life. I participate in the process—dating, attending church events, proactively putting myself in places where single men are found, and even joining online dating services. (I almost wish I sat on my hands before enduring that last one!) As time moves by and my desires remain unmet, I start to question God. Just like Sarah, I blame him. Then, I take matters into my own hands. I lower my standards just to be in a relationship. It's not happening fast enough, so I decide to settle because I'm over thirty and single.

When we make choices to accept less than what God has for us, we are shortsighted. We rob ourselves of the joy God intends for our lives. We may feel like God is silent during a season of our life and that he's not answering our prayers. These feelings are based on the plans *we* have for *our* lives—the ones we create for ourselves, either consciously or subconsciously. God's will for our lives is so much greater than we ever dare to hope. He knows us better than we know ourselves.

> Perhaps God's timing is different from yours, but that doesn't mean anything is wrong with you. I know so many incredible people who are single.
>
> —Ally, 34, married

In Sarah's story, the situation worsened as she experienced the consequences of her decisions. Sarah's maidservant Hagar became pregnant by Abraham, and Sarah lashed out at her husband and blamed him for her suffering (see Genesis 16:5). Sarah continued to spiral downward. She tormented Hagar, and the woman ended up running away in despair. As Sarah experienced the consequences of her sin, she became miserable. This wasn't God's best plan for Sarah's life.

But God didn't forget Sarah. Through it all, he still loved her and didn't give up on her. In the same way, he doesn't give up on us when we make mistakes and fail to trust him. I imagine God is saddened when we settle for less than everything he wants to give us. We're his children, and he wants the best for us.

Even after Sarah made a mess of the situation, God kept his promises: "I will bless her and will surely give you a son by her. I will bless her so that she will be the mother of nations; kings of peoples will come from her" (Genesis 17:16).

What was Abraham's response to this declaration that Sarah would have a son? He fell to the ground laughing because Sarah was ninety years old at the time. A little while later, Sarah heard the news from the Lord. What was her response? She laughed too. However, God didn't see much humor in the situation:

Then the LORD said to Abraham, "Why did Sarah laugh and say, 'Will I really have a child, now that I am old?' Is anything too hard for the LORD? I will return to you at the appointed time next year, and Sarah will have a son." (Genesis 18:13-14)

"Is anything too hard for the Lord?" How would it revolutionize your daily life if you truly believed nothing is impossible for God? When I start getting excited about God's plan for my life and accept it as the plan I want above all else, then I can peacefully wait on the Lord.

Trusting God's plan for my life means I have less anxiety on a daily basis. I live in the present moment instead of always worrying about the future. God can use me today for his kingdom. I don't want to waste the opportunity to serve him because I'm so busy planning my future marriage and children.

Thankfully, this part of Sarah's story had a happy ending with the birth of Isaac. From the beginning of time, God's plan included the birth of Isaac. The end of this story was never in doubt. Neither is the end of your story—it's part of God's sovereign plan.

Sarah and Abraham had doubts. They believed they were too old to be used by God. Sarah believed God had forgotten about her. She thought God refused to answer her pleas for children. She laughed at God.

I also have doubts. Many times, I believe God has forgotten me. I get so frustrated with my singleness I want to laugh. It's not the kind of laughter that brings joy, but the same type of laughter Sarah expressed. It's the laughter of one who has given up and believes it's too late.

The Bible tells us Isaac's birth happened "at the very time God had promised him" (Genesis 21:2). God wants you to trust in him, to desire "his good, pleasing and perfect will" (Romans 12:2). God knows what you need. It's up to you to submit your fears to him, lay down your plans at his feet, and accept the contentment that he wants to bring into your life.

Truth: God does not forget his children.

Even though we sometimes feel forgotten, God is present. He doesn't overlook his promises to us. My mind struggles to comprehend God's ways, especially when he allows things to happen that I don't understand. When my boyfriend rejected me and chose someone else, I started to question every part of my life. We only see a small piece of the puzzle—today. God has the benefit of seeing the whole picture—our entire future. He often uses unmet desires and times of loneliness to make us more like him. He teaches us to wait on him and his timing.

Remember the heartbroken twenty-four-year-old version of me? At the time, I truly believed God made a big mistake by letting my boyfriend choose someone else. Now, I understand God showed me grace. The event that triggered so much despair in my life was actually an act of grace—one that prevented an even bigger disaster. In hindsight, I can see that God was shaping me. Leslie Haskin says, "You are today who you are because of every person, every experience, and every thought God has allowed and connected to bring about His redemption plan in your life. *Perfect.*"[1]

Instead of abandoning me, God actually protected me. I don't always understand God's ways, but I trust his faithfulness.

A Faithful God

As I look back at Sarah's story in Genesis and my own story from more than ten years ago, the faithfulness of God is evident. Even when we fail to trust him, his sovereign plan is not in question. I like the advice Nancy Wilson gives to unmarried women. "An unmarried woman is to have a high view of marriage, but she is also to have a high view of God's sovereignty in her own life."[2]

> And by faith even Sarah, who was past childbearing age, was enabled to bear children because she considered him faithful who had made the promise.
> (Hebrews 11:11)

This past year, I chose to participate in two silent retreats. I visited two different monasteries and entered into a few days of complete silence on each trip. I wanted to hear God. We fill our lives with so much noise—television, radio, iPods, Internet, Facebook, Twitter, and so on. Even time spent volunteering at church and squeezing in daily quiet times may represent ways to stay busy and check more items off the list. We are busy and noisy. How does God compete with all of that sound? He doesn't. He won't shout over the clamor. He waits for us to become quiet and turn to him.

Removing the noise from my life felt strange. At first, I felt jumpy and nervous with the silence. Then, my introverted heart started craving it. I turned to God and asked him to speak to me in the silence. Instead of answering all my questions about circumstances, he began to show me his character.

No matter how much I learn about God, the knowledge cannot even scratch the surface of his holy character. Who can truly understand the depths of his love, faithfulness, and holiness? It reaches to the skies! And our God in his infinite holiness and faithfulness is the same God who cares about each of us. He cares about every single thought, each painful moment, and all the heartbreak you have experienced. The Bible even tells us that God holds on to your tears: "You keep track of all my sorrows. You have collected all my tears in your bottle. You have recorded each one in your book" (Psalm 56:8, NLT).

Also, if you have accepted Jesus as your Savior, God's Spirit lives inside of you. Even though I'm broken and sinful, God chooses to place his Spirit within me. When I consider how the Creator of all—the most holy one—gives me a piece of his living Spirit, I understand how much God loves me and will never forget me.

Have you ever come across a passage that seems to answer every question? For me, that passage is the following:

Yet this I call to mind and therefore I have hope: Because of the LORD's great love we are not consumed, for his compassions never fail. They are new every morning; great is your faithfulness. I say to myself,

> Regardless of whether you are married or single, God hasn't forgotten about you. You are precious to him.
>
> —*Catherine, 45, married*

"The LORD is my portion; therefore I will wait for him." (Lamentations 3:21-24)

Each time I begin saying, "But, God . . . ," a part of this passage provides the answer.

But, God . . . I am lonely. *I am your portion.*

But, God . . . when am I going to get married? *My faithfulness is great.*

But, God . . . I am truly sad. *I love you; you will not be consumed.*

But, God . . . each day seems to get harder. *My compassion renews every morning.*

But, God . . . I'm not sure how much longer I can wait. *Wait for me.*

God speaks to us through his words in the Bible. He is faithful and responds to our fears and questions.

I like the way my friend Catherine sums up God's faithfulness: The Lord knows everything about you and your future. Talk with him. Be completely honest—even when you are angry. He already knows. Also, write out remembrances of his faithfulness: when someone complimented you, the first daffodil of the season, extra money when you needed it, a friend's kind words. All of these things are for you—personally directed to you. Focus on him. Understand what love really is.

—*Catherine, 45, married*

A Trustworthy God

Even though I realize God is faithful, I still have trust issues. Do you sometimes worry God won't come through for you? He comes through for others, but what about you? At times, I struggle with apprehensions and fear God won't meet the desires of my heart.

When I attended my first silent retreat, God showed his presence in a big way. At this particular retreat, we were led by a counselor in spiritual direction for one hour each day. There were four women on the weekend retreat. Before arriving at the monastery, I knew none of them. As soon as we met each other, we immediately entered into our silent time.

I passed one woman in the hall and smiled. I met another on the hiking trails and waved, suppressing my first instinct to yell, "Hi, there!" Instead of speaking aloud, I started praying silently for each woman as I saw her around the monastic campus.

As I walked out to a swing by the pond to spend some quiet time, I noticed one woman from our group sitting on a blanket by the water. Because of the beautiful scene, I took out my camera and captured a quick photo. I sat down to begin reading the Bible. Instead, my mind kept wandering. It continued to dwell on the woman I photographed by the pond. I knew her name was Jamie but not much more. A verse immediately came to my mind: "The LORD will fight for you; you need only to be still" (Exodus 14:14).

As I attempted to concentrate on my prayer time, Jamie and this verse lingered in my thoughts. Later that night, I decided to make a card for Jamie. I wrote the verse on a note card and anonymously slipped it under the door to her room.

At the end of the retreat, the four women and our director came back together to share how God spoke to us. During our time together, I discovered my note to Jamie had some divine implications.

When Jamie first received the note under her door, she wasn't sure who placed it there. When I explained how I saw her sitting by the water and took the photograph, she was stunned. I told her the particular verse on that card came to my mind while I watched her sitting by the pond. With tears streaming, she told me she was studying Exodus 14:14—the very same verse—at the exact moment I saw her and took the picture.

The moment is only explained by God's presence and direction. God loves Jamie so much that he emphasized his willingness to fight for her. God loves me so much that he allowed me to deliver part of his message to Jamie and share that moment with her.

> Let us hold tightly without wavering to the hope we affirm, for God can be trusted to keep his promise. (Hebrews 10:23, NLT)

When I experience God like this, it reminds me that he loves us more than we can imagine. In that infinite love, he created a plan for each of us. We can trust that God will show up. Believe anything is possible with God. He is trustworthy. He will fight for you. He will not forget you.

● ● ●

So be strong and courageous! Do not be afraid and do not panic before them. For the LORD your God will personally go ahead of you. He will neither fail you nor abandon you.
(Deuteronomy 31:6, NLT)

God has forgotten about me.

Women who believe this lie often say:

- God must be too busy to worry about me.
- I feel abandoned.
- God doesn't care about my happiness.
- I can't trust God.
- I'm tired of waiting on God to answer my prayers.

God does not forget his children.

God says:

- **I will always be with you.**
  And surely I am with you always, to the very end of the age. (Matthew 28:20b)
- **I am faithful.**
  For great is your love, higher than the heavens; your faithfulness reaches to the skies. (Psalm 108:4)
- **I am trustworthy.**
  Sovereign Lord, you are God! Your covenant is trustworthy, and you have promised these good things to your servant. (2 Samuel 7:28)
- **I care about you.**
  Praise be to the God and Father of our Lord Jesus Christ, the Father of compassion and the God of all comfort, who comforts us in all our troubles, so that we can comfort those in any trouble with the comfort we ourselves receive from God. (2 Corinthians 1:3-4)
- **I will fight for you.**
  The Lord will fight for you; you need only to be still. (Exodus 14:14)

Lies I Believe:

....

....

....

....

....

....

....

....

Truth I Want to Remember:

....

....

....

....

....

....

....

....

....

Lie #3: Sex outside of marriage is okay.

All alone in my bed, I stared at the ceiling as tears ran down my cheeks. The front door slammed as he stormed out. I recalled the harsh words he just spat at me. "This is ridiculous. We've been dating for over a year and you're still holding out on me. What's wrong with you? None of your friends act like this. You're the only one who wants to wait until marriage. It's ridiculous at your age."

My apologies no longer worked. I realized it was my fault. I understood his concerns. His words became part of me, and I believed I was acting unreasonably. I internalized everything he said, but I still wouldn't have sex with him. I didn't completely respect myself, but I also understood this wasn't the loving scenario I had always imagined.

Finally, I shared the destructive pattern of the relationship with a good friend. She looked stunned, but she spoke truth to me. "He's lying to you. He's manipulating you. You deserve better than that. You deserve to be respected by the person you are dating."

I had fallen into the trap of believing the lies. From reading God's Word, I knew that sexual immorality was improper, and I tried to obey—but for all the wrong reasons. I wanted to wait until marriage to have sex, but it was just a rule to me. I didn't truly understand why God wanted me to wait. If I did, I would have been much bolder in my stance. If I truly understood God's best plan for me, I wouldn't have dated someone like him in the first place.

Let's be honest. I haven't always made the right decisions about guarding my heart and protecting my body. The chapter following this one will address God's redeeming grace for those times when we mess up. I'm definitely not claiming to be an expert on either side of this issue. That's why I have interviewed and surveyed many women for this chapter—married and single, those who had sex outside of marriage and those who waited.

The lie is a destructive one. "It's okay for me to have sex outside of marriage." Society wants you to believe it. Satan wants you to believe it. Some of your friends want you to believe it. Sometimes, you want to believe it.

Our enemy uses many avenues to convince us this lie is true: insecurity, peer pressure, our culture, loneliness, anxiety, physical needs, movies, television, and many more.

Consider the many versions of lies wrapped up in the topic of sex outside of marriage:[1]

- No one waits until marriage to have sex.
- You should have sex with someone before you marry him.
- Sex is no big deal.
- The purpose of sex is my pleasure.
- It will be boring to have sex with just one man for the rest of my life.
- God doesn't expect me to wait for marriage if I'm over the age of thirty.
- Sex will make me feel loved.
- Sex outside of marriage is okay as long as we love each other.
- I won't feel lonely anymore if I have sex.
- Sex is the only way to keep a man interested in me.

Yet God says to you:

- Do not have sex outside of marriage.

"But among you there must not be even a hint of sexual immorality, or of any kind of impurity, or of greed, because these are improper for God's holy people" (Ephesians 5:3).

- Flee from sexual immorality.

  "Flee from sexual immorality. All other sins a person commits are outside the body, but whoever sins sexually, sins against their own body" (1 Corinthians 6:18).

- Your body is a temple of the Holy Spirit.

  "Do you not know that your bodies are temples of the Holy Spirit, who is in you, whom you have received from God? You are not your own; you were bought at a price. Therefore honor God with your bodies" (1 Corinthians 6:19-20).

- Marriage is sacred.

  "Marriage should be honored by all, and the marriage bed kept pure, for God will judge the adulterer and all the sexually immoral" (Hebrews 13:4).

- You must protect your heart.

  "Above all else, guard your heart, for everything you do flows from it" (Proverbs 4:23).

- You are valuable.

  "Look at the birds. They don't plant or harvest or store food in barns, for your heavenly Father feeds them. And aren't you far more valuable to him than they are?" (Matthew 6:26, NLT).

- You must trust me.

  "'For I know the plans I have for you,' declares the LORD, 'plans to prosper you and not to harm you, plans to give you hope and a future'" (Jeremiah 29:11).

- I know what is best for you.

  "It is God's will that you should be sanctified: that you should avoid sexual immorality" (1 Thessalonians 4:3).

- I love you.

  "But God demonstrates his own love for us in this: While we were still sinners, Christ died for us" (Romans 5:8).

Truth: God commands us to flee from sexual immorality and to keep sex within the covenant of marriage.

The commandments God set in the Bible aren't for his benefit. They aren't in place for him to sit on his throne and look down on us, just waiting for us to mess up. Even though we sometimes view God as the cosmic judge, jury, and jailer, this perspective is flawed.

God loves us so much he wants us to have as little pain and heartbreak as possible. He sets up best practices that, if followed, will protect our hearts. Obviously, bad things still happen. I'm not advocating you'll have a nice, happy life with no pain if you follow God's rules. We still live in a broken world. But I'm confident your life will have less self-inflicted pain if you attempt to follow God's outline for life.

> Pray. Seek God. Listen and trust what you hear from him. God has grown me so much in the years that I've been single. He has drawn me to him and allowed me to seriously seek and follow him. He has taken me places I don't think I would have gone had I been in a relationship. He has truly shown me what it is to be a living sacrifice.
>
> —Jordan, 31, single

Unfortunately, our brokenness often clouds our judgment in the area of sex. Rebellion is sometimes a product of our own broken homes. Some of us look for love in the wrong places to fill an emotional void.

Angela gives an example of this:

I did not see any examples of true abstinence. Plus, because of insecurities from my childhood, I was desperate for love and used sex to try and meet that need. I gave into temptation, ultimately believing the lie that nobody really waits until they are married.

—*Angela, 30, married*

Never once have I heard someone say, "I shouldn't have waited. I wish I'd engaged in premarital sex." But I hear the opposite very frequently. I hear the regret, sometimes the shame, expressed about not waiting. Even where God has healed and forgiven (and he will), there are still consequences to our actions.

I had to tell him before we got married that I didn't save myself for him—the one true love of my life. I didn't have that gift to give him. I hated that conversation. Sometimes I have flashbacks to what I did. Satan uses it to attack my self-esteem—"Why should the Lord use you? You couldn't even wait to get married."

—*Catherine, 45, married*

• • •

He told me he had waited for me and I was sad that I couldn't say the same (he already knew this about me). It was difficult for me to think I had hurt him on our wedding night—he was presenting me the greatest gift ever and I couldn't do the same for him. He was very understanding and tender with me, but it was difficult nonetheless.

—*Abigail, 48, married*

• • •

It isn't secret knowledge but rather a piece of yourself that is given away to someone. You can't reclaim it. You are forever tied to that person in a deep way.

—*Lydia, 40, single*

• • •

I interviewed more than thirty women about sex before marriage and asked them, "Is there any advice you would like to give unmarried women about sex outside of marriage?" Here are some of their beautiful and encouraging responses.

It is definitely better to wait until marriage! Marriage has lots of difficulties, but waiting is one way for you to work on your marriage before you ever get married. If you already have done things you wish you hadn't, . . . start again fresh today. Pray for the Lord to take away those memories and wipe you white as snow and then start again. Walk forward in purity and save yourself for your husband. It will help when you have no other thoughts of other guys in your sex life with your husband. It will give your husband more confidence. Satan would love to have you compare your husband to other guys; staying pure is just one more way to evict Satan from that area of your life.

—Jill, 32, married

• • •

It's complicated enough within a committed relationship; why make it so difficult for yourself by having sex with someone you are not sure about? It's not worth it. Save yourself the trouble and the regrets.

—Greta, 30, married

• • •

Wait. It will be worth it. I had sex outside of marriage, and I fear it won't be the same with my future husband. I encourage you to wait and share that beautiful experience with one another as God intended it to be.

—Alexis, 29, single

• • •

Do not have sex until you are married. It's very hard to undo memories and past experiences once you have them. God will greatly bless your obedience in this.

—Rachel, 34, married

• • •

It is really worth it to wait. It makes things so much less complicated. You also don't have to live in fear of consequences, and you know that the person you are with is with you because of you, not for what you give them.

—*Jennifer, 38, married*

• • •

If you haven't had sex yet, please don't outside of marriage. You have something to give your husband that no one else has had. That is a precious gift. You are worth the wait. You may feel like you are the only one, but you aren't. Keep trusting in the Lord. Doing what he commands is far better than anything else. Be particular about who you date and who you kiss. If you have had sex, you can be forgiven. Don't continue on that path; get out of the relationship and determine not to do it again. Pray; realize your worth through God's eyes, not through man's eyes. The God of heaven and earth has redeemed you. You are his priceless princess.

—*Catherine, 45, married*

• • •

I also surveyed a group of single and recently married men. Fifty percent of the men who responded admitted they have believed the lie that having sex outside of marriage is okay. The lie is a prevalent one, but here are some of their honest opinions about premarital sex.

[Sex is] an important symbol of a sacred bond.

—*Nate, 30, single*

• • •

[Premarital sex] wreaks havoc and complicates the dating process (i.e., unplanned pregnancy, negative emotions) and can hinder the blessings God could have on the spiritual relationship of the couple.

—*Jake, 36, single*

• • •

In this day and age where unrestricted sexual expression is promoted as a moral good, taking a stand to remain celibate until marriage is a way to loudly proclaim by example what we believe to be true.

—Caleb, 37, married

• • •

(Additional quotes from men regarding the topic of premarital sex are included in the bonus section, "Single Men Respond.")

• • •

In her book *Wait for Me: Rediscovering the Joy of Purity in Romance*, Rebecca St. James gives this helpful advice:
The only way that we can resist the desire to sin is by relying on God's strength. I would encourage you to turn to God and pray for His power to stand strong. The only way to live a life of purity is through God's power![2]

Joseph's Story

In the book of Genesis, we find a biblical example of someone who lived a life of purity through God's power. Joseph suffered through some difficult circumstances early in his life. Things finally started turning around for him when a man named Potiphar put Joseph in charge of his household. Genesis 39:6 reads that Joseph was "well-built and handsome." His boss's wife noticed this and said to Joseph, "Come to bed with me!" (v. 7).

Things were different back in the days of Joseph. I'm sure his life looked a lot different from our lives. But this straightforward story sounds like a scene from a current-day television drama. God empowered Joseph to resist temptation and wrote an ending that is much more pure than many things we see on television these days.

Joseph refused Potiphar's wife. He told her that his boss "withheld nothing from me except you, because you are his wife." He asked a very important question. "How then could I do such a wicked thing and sin against God?" (Genesis 39:9).

Joseph recognized this sin would be a sin against God. It would also be a sin against Potiphar and against Joseph's own body, but Joseph respected God enough to understand that sin is truly an act against God.[3]

I remember the first time I understood this principle. I became heartbroken over my sin. Even if I don't respect myself or others enough to resist temptation, I respect God. I must repent to God first, turn from that sin, and then seek out others to make restitution. First and foremost, my sin is a sin against God. It's a sobering thought and one that I strive to consider before giving in to temptation.

In the midst of temptation by Potiphar's wife, Joseph kept out of her way as much as possible. He attempted to remove himself from the situation. He continued to perform his job duties, but he avoided Potiphar's wife. When he did encounter her, it didn't go very well:

> One day he went into the house to attend to his duties, and none of the household servants was inside. She caught him by his cloak and said, "Come to bed with me!" But he left his cloak in her hand and ran out of the house. (Genesis 39:11-12)

He "ran out of the house." He fled sexual immorality. If you're familiar with this story, you know Joseph paid a price for his values. He ended up in jail for a crime he didn't commit, but he won the battle in God's eyes.

The picture of Joseph fleeing stays in my mind. It's tempting to push the limits and stay in a dangerous situation. We rationalize and say, "I can control myself. I'm not sinning by just being here." No, I may not be sinning yet. But each small step toward a sinful situation is a step away from God's protection.

Consider the wise advice in Proverbs: "Give careful thought to the paths for your feet and be steadfast in all your ways. Do not turn to the right or the left; keep your foot from evil" (4:26-27).

How do we stay diligent in our faith and maintain our values? How do we keep our feet from evil? We take steps to remove ourselves from tempting situations. We control the types of images we put into our brains. We dwell on pure and good things. We find good friends to hold us accountable. We date well and ensure our partners have the same values. But we can't do it alone. Ultimately, we must rely on God to shepherd us in this area.

> Tell God every time you hurt. Be who God designed you to be. Live like you want the guy whom you'll marry to live. If you don't want him to smoke, don't smoke. If you want him to save sex for you, then save yourself for him.
>
> —Marie, 51, married

God as Shepherd

As we continue to look to God's character for answers, we find important perspective by viewing God as our Shepherd. In our culture, this example seems a little outdated. I don't know any current-day shepherds. I'm sure they still exist somewhere in the world.

Most of us know that a shepherd protects and provides care for a flock of sheep. Consider this example from the book of Genesis when Jacob arrives at a new land during his journey:

> There [Jacob] saw a well in the open country, with three flocks of sheep lying near it because the flocks were watered from that well. The stone over the mouth of the well was large. When all the flocks were gathered there, the shepherds would roll the stone away from the well's mouth and water the sheep. Then they would return the stone to its place over the mouth of the well. (Genesis 29:2-3)

A shepherd desires to protect his sheep. Similar to the shepherds caring for their sheep in this passage, our Shepherd—God—desires to protect us. As sheep, we don't always know what is best for our lives. Why did the shepherds place the stone over the mouth of the well in this story?

Maybe the sheep would come back all day long and keep drinking the water. Or maybe they would try to get water and drown in the well. Without the protection of the shepherd, a sheep may drink too much water, consume contaminated water, or drown in the water. In the same way, God shepherds us for our protection.

Sex is a good thing. God created it. He determined sex within the covenant of marriage to be the best outcome for his sheep. Marriage is also a good thing. God knows that marriage to the wrong person will be hurtful and damaging. He desires to shepherd us along the right path—to protect us from choosing a path that leads to poor consequences.

So, God asks us to keep the stone in place—to keep ourselves pure and save sex for marriage. It's never too late to heed the Shepherd's advice. He guides us along the right paths, the ones that bring honor to his name, and thankfully, his mercies are new every morning.

• • •

The LORD is my shepherd;
I have all that I need.
He lets me rest in green meadows;
he leads me beside peaceful streams.
He renews my strength.
He guides me along right paths,
bringing honor to his name.
(Psalm 23:1-3, NLT)

Sex outside of marriage is okay.

Women who believe this lie often say:
• No one waits until marriage to have sex.
• Surely God doesn't expect me to wait any longer.
• It's okay to have sex when I'm in love.
• Oral sex doesn't count as sex.
• I need to know whether the sex is good before I marry him.
• I've already messed up, so I'll keep having sex.

God commands us to flee from sexual immorality and keep sex within the covenant of marriage.

God says:
• **Save all types of sex for marriage.**
  But among you there must not be even a hint of sexual immorality, or of any kind of impurity. (Ephesians 5:3)
• **Protect your heart.**
  Guard your heart, for everything you do flows from it. (Proverbs 4:23)
• **Let me work out my will in your life.**
  So let God work his will in you. . . . Quit dabbling in sin. Purify your inner life. Quit playing the field. Hit bottom, and cry your eyes out. The fun and games are over. Get serious, really serious. Get down on your knees before the Master; it's the only way you'll get on your feet. (James 4:7-10, TM)
• **I am your Shepherd.**
  He tends his flock like a shepherd: He gathers the lambs in his arms and carries them close to his heart. (Isaiah 40:11)

Lies I Believe:

....

....

....

....

....

....

....

....

Truth I Want to Remember:

....

....

....

....

....

....

....

....

Lie #4: My past can't be forgiven.

I once spent a weekend in jail." Those were the first words I ever heard Reese speak. Since we were in the middle of a preparatory meeting for a short-term mission trip, I was a little shocked. Who puts something like that out there for a roomful of almost strangers to hear? Although I'm ashamed to admit it, part of me immediately judged Reese. Her transparency scared me, and I was pretty sure we were too different to become close friends.

One of my favorite things about God is his tendency to throw surprises into our lives along the way. Contrary to my first instincts, Reese and I have indeed become lifelong friends. God often uses her words to speak truth into my life. I love her dearly, and I admire her boldness in spite of some awful circumstances. Let's back up, though. On a train ride through the countryside during our mission trip, Reese told me her story.[1]

She grew up going to church every Sunday in a small community. Reese said, "We looked like a typical, churchgoing family." In reality, her life at home was far from ideal. Reese admits, "Growing up, I lived in fear. There was a lot of anger in my home, and I witnessed physical abuse. I was scared, but I didn't tell anyone what was happening."

Instead, Reese suffered emotional scars and started believing the lies she continuously heard in her mind: "You're ugly. You're fat. You're not worth anything." In her search for value and acceptance, Reese ended up turning to alcohol. "I started drinking as a teenager. It continued through college and for years afterward."

"I've tried most everything to drown the pain," Reese explained. Desperately searching for something to make her feel whole, she gave herself away to whiskey, drugs, and men. She only accumulated more shame and brokenness.

One night about ten years ago, she met a guy who made her feel special and valuable. Reese was smitten. She easily took on his party lifestyle and ended up stranded in a bar one night all alone. Although she doesn't remember what happened next, she got in her car and started driving the wrong direction on the interstate. While blacked out from the alcohol, Reese had a head-on collision with a family of three.

It's difficult for her to talk about the accident. Miraculously, no one was injured. "I remember waking up in the backseat of a police car, spitting out a mouthful of broken glass," Reese recalled. "I was ashamed and horrified." She was convicted of a DUI and spent the weekend in jail. Reese hit rock bottom, but the accident changed her life.

"Jesus became real to me in the days after the accident. He saved me because I'm worth fighting for. When I realized God loved me and wanted me, I knew it was the acceptance I had longed for my whole life." Reese's relationship with God changed after the accident, and she became passionate about following him.

Reese told me Psalm 32 has been crucial in her healing process and also gave her the courage to tell her story.

Blessed is the one whose transgressions are forgiven, whose sins are covered. Blessed is the one whose sin the LORD does not count against them and in whose spirit is no deceit. *When I kept silent, my bones wasted away through my groaning all day long.* (Psalm 32:1-3, emphasis mine)

Reese's transgressions are forgiven, and her sins are covered. When she found the verses above, she knew she couldn't keep silent. She had to tell others about the redeeming love and forgiveness of God. Although she has traveled across the world telling her story and proclaiming the goodness of God, sometimes Reese still struggles with guilt and remembering her past. Listening to Reese tell her story reminds me of the times when I allow guilt and lies to overtake me.

Mornings are tough for me. I'm definitely not a morning person, but it's more than that. When I first wake up, the lies bombard me. During that vulnerable time between sleeping and fully awake, Satan hits me with some of his best shots. "You are a loser. You're all alone. Do you really think God would use someone like you?" Many times, I recall sins from my past. Satan whispers, "What kind of Christian are you? Do you really think God can forgive *that* sin?" Many people would label this spiritual warfare. Regardless of what you call it, the battle is real.

> Fight to believe the truth and not lies. God's voice is uplifting, encouraging, loving, and life-giving.
>
> —Jill, 32, married

I know God has a plan for my life. But, what if I messed it up? Have I missed my chance? I fear that my mistakes have doomed me to a life of singleness, although my heart still desires marriage and children. So, I replay all the missed chances in my head. It doesn't matter whether I broke up with the guy or he left me. Either way, I find a way to blame myself. If I had responded differently, would he have stayed? Should I have chosen him, even though I knew I was settling?

The message of this chapter is so important to me. If I had to choose only one chapter for a single woman to read, it would be this one.

Truth: God will redeem your past and your mistakes.

*Y*ou are never too far from the reach of God. By dying on the cross, Jesus paid the price for 100 percent of the sins every person has committed. He victoriously rose from the grave for the benefit of every single person. Even though he knew that some would reject him and never accept his gift, he chose to die in spite of that rejection.

Everything that needs to be done for your salvation has already been accomplished. All you need to do is respond to the gift he extends. He knocks at the door. You only need to answer.

Once we have accepted his gift, we don't have to continue punishing ourselves for the past. I learned this the hard way. Grace was not a concept I easily received. The Bible proclaims that God forgives me. I had to learn to forgive myself and release myself from the debt that held me captive.

It's interesting that Psalm 32, the same passage that spoke to Reese, addresses the guilt we feel. Although the verses specifically declare our sins are covered and our transgressions are forgiven, it gives another piece of hope. In verse 5, we learn that after confessing our transgressions to the Lord, he will forgive "the guilt of [our] sin." Not just the sin, but the *guilt* of it as well.

This message is crucial for our generation. Many of us grew up in an environment like the one in which I was raised—one that emphasized performance and was short on grace. Be a good girl. Keep the rules and act nicely. Only then will you be rewarded. If you act ugly, you will be punished. Good equals love. Bad equals rejection. Guilt thrives in this conditional environment.

The biggest lesson I learned about grace came from a pastor, Carter Crenshaw. He taught me that nothing I do will make God love me more, and nothing I do will make God love me less. At first, it made absolutely no sense to me. Isn't God happy when I do good things? Isn't God sad when I fall short?

The point is that God's unconditional and perfect love is already at its maximum capacity. It's a love bigger than I can comprehend with my human brain.

> We can never measure up or do enough for God, but that is why Christ died for us. We need to concentrate on *being* instead of *doing*, specifically being content whatever our circumstances and knowing that we are perfected in Christ.
>
> —Anne, 28, married

Doing something good won't increase this love. Doing something bad won't decrease it. It's already perfect, full, and unchanging.

God accepts me. I am broken, and my sin is ugly. Regardless, God accepts me because his love is not based on what I do—it's based on the character of God and who *he* is.

For so long, the good little girl inside of me tried to keep the ugliness hidden. If I can just go to church enough, God will love me. If I can volunteer, teach Sunday school, serve at vacation Bible school, pray, read the Bible, tithe (performance, performance, performance), then God will see that I'm worthy.

I failed to understand the most important concept. God doesn't love me because I *do*. God loves me because I *am*. Resting in that truth saved me. It saved me from the cycle of attempting to earn God's love, respect, and forgiveness. God didn't need me to earn salvation. He sent Jesus to earn it for me.

You may be thinking, "Yeah, but she doesn't know what I've done. My past is too ugly. I'm too broken. All of that grace stuff is for people who commit little sins. My sins are too big."

Let me say this boldly: God is big enough. He knows all about your past and your sins, and his love has not diminished one millimeter due to that knowledge. He loves you and accepts you. He patiently waits at the door for you to invite him into your life.

God as Redeemer

I like the analogy my friend James uses to describe God as our Redeemer. Imagine that someone is certain you have a police record. He is determined to make your record publicly known. He goes to the head of law enforcement, the chief of police, and asks about your record of offenses. However, the chief of police responds, "There is no record of any wrongdoing."

If you have accepted the free gift of salvation God provides through Jesus, your sins have been forgiven and erased. Jesus stands there as our chief of police, saying, "There is no record of this sin." The Bible tells us that God doesn't even remember our sins: "For I will forgive their wickedness and will remember their sins no more" (Jeremiah 31:34b).

God doesn't get exasperated with us. In our human minds, we sometimes picture him standing there with hands on hips, his finger pointed in our face. Sometimes, we assign the frustration we heard in our earthly father's voice to God. If you learned to walk on eggshells around your earthly father, you may believe you have to act the same way with God.

Let me give you another picture of our heavenly Father to replace that image in your head. I know this story is very familiar and you might be tempted to skip ahead since you've heard it many times. But I want you to look past the surface aspects of the parable and focus on the characteristics of the Father.

In the gospel of Luke, Jesus tells us the story of a father with two sons. The younger son asked for his share of the father's estate (while the father was still living) and then ran off. Luke 15:13 tells us the younger son "squandered his wealth in wild living." We're left to imagine his "wild living" included a lot of sinning. He thought only of himself and didn't worry about how his actions affected his father or anyone else. I can think of a few times when that described my actions as well. I imagine regret and guilt were well-known companions to him. Sound familiar?

When the money ran out and the parties ended, the young man came to his senses and realized he had "sinned against heaven" and against his father (Luke 15:21). He decided to go home.

Let's not skip over this important decision. He could have remained with the pigs in the field where he was working. He could have embraced self-pity and remained with his friends named regret and guilt. Instead, he was brave. He chose to go home and confess.

If you're like me, you may be imagining a scenario where you have to tell your father how you wasted your entire share of the inheritance. Maybe you've actually had to face your dad and admit some shameful things that disappointed him. Maybe that's why it's hard for you to imagine God extending unconditional love. Or maybe that's why it's easy for you.

In this parable, we know the father represents God. Let's see how he responded to his son coming home: "But while he was still a long way off, his father saw him and was filled with compassion for him; *he ran to his son*, threw his arms around him and kissed him" (Luke 15:20, emphasis mine).

Have you ever pictured God running? God is sovereign over space and time. He doesn't have to run. But he runs when his children come home. Regardless of what you've done. No matter how long you've been gone. God runs to you. As I write these words, tears pour down my face because his grace still overwhelms me. His love, in spite of my sin, is unconditional. All we have to do is come home.

Do you believe your actions have put you outside of God's reach? God's love for you is constant, no matter what you do. You are never outside the reach of God's redeeming grace.

God as Healer

God's redemption doesn't end with forgiveness. Maybe you've already come home and accepted God's forgiveness, but your wounds are still hurting. You know you're forgiven by God, but you haven't released yourself from the debt. You can't let the past go.

I wholeheartedly believe God forgives us and also wants to heal us. He longs to set you free of the burden you're carrying. Psalm 103 is one of my favorites. It's about redemption, forgiveness, and healing.

Praise the LORD, my soul, and forget not his benefits—who forgives all your sins and heals all your diseases, who redeems your life from the pit and crowns you with love and compassion. (Psalm 103:2-4)

In order for God to be our Healer, we have to release the past to him. Oswald Chambers wrote, "Our yesterdays hold broken and irreversible things for us. It is true that we have lost opportunities that will never return, but God can transform this destructive anxiety into a constructive thoughtfulness for the future. Let the past rest, but let it rest in the sweet embrace of Christ."[2]

We need to let our regrets rest with God so we can live in the present. We also must release our future to him. I struggle with believing my mistakes have doomed my future. I worry I've missed the chance to fulfill my hopes to be a wife and mother. I don't know what the future holds, but I know God has promised to make something beautiful from the ashes of my past. If I turn everything over to him, God will "bestow on them a crown of beauty instead of ashes, the oil of joy instead of mourning, and a garment of praise instead of a spirit of despair" (Isaiah 61:3).

I can't think of anything better than the ashes of my past being used for something beautiful.

Proof of God's Redemption

Just in case you need further proof of God's redemptive power, I want to show you something. I love that the Bible is full of people like you and me—imperfect people with colorful pasts. God specially selected people to be the ancestors of his Son, Jesus. It would have been so easy for him to choose the most righteous and noble people in the Bible for the lineage of his Son.

Instead, God chose to give us one more example of his forgiveness and mercy. Take a look at these excerpts from the genealogy of Jesus, as recorded in the gospel of Matthew: "Abraham was the father of Isaac, Isaac the father of Jacob, Jacob the father of Judah and his brothers, Judah the father of Perez and Zerah, whose mother was Tamar" (1:2-3).

Let's pause here for a moment. Normally, only the names of men appear, but Tamar is the first woman mentioned in the lineage. It seems important solely because of that. It's also significant because Tamar wasn't exactly the model of purity and innocence. In Genesis 38, we learn that Tamar was a widow. After her mother-in-law passed away, she disguised herself, pretending to be a prostitute, and slept with her father-in-law, Judah. She became pregnant from this union and gave birth to the twins mentioned in the lineage of Christ.

Let's move on to the next woman mentioned in the family tree: "Salmon the father of Boaz, whose mother was Rahab" (Matthew 1:5).

By now, I bet you've guessed that Rahab was another woman with some sin in her past. In the book of Joshua, we learn that Rahab was a prostitute who lived in Jericho. She hid and protected two Israelite spies and ended up making a deal with them. She asked for her life to be spared as reward for protecting them because she believed that God had already given the land to the Israelites. Joshua kept his promise of protection to Rahab, and she came to live with the Israelites after Jericho was conquered and burned.

There is another woman who is not specifically named in the genealogy of Jesus, but we are given enough information to know her identity: "David was the father of Solomon, whose mother had been Uriah's wife" (Matthew 1:6).

We know that Solomon was the son of David and Bathsheba, formerly the wife of Uriah. Most of us know this story well. While Uriah was away serving in the army, King David slept with Bathsheba (see 2 Samuel 11). After David learned Bathsheba was pregnant, he gave instructions for Uriah to be placed on the front lines of the battlefield. When Uriah died, David married Bathsheba.

Jesus, our Savior, was a descendant of deception, prostitution, and adultery. And it appears that God went out of his way to make sure these women were mentioned in the recorded genealogy.

We serve a God who is all about redemption. It wasn't enough for him to send his Son into the world to provide a means of salvation. Through the lineage of Christ, he also gave us a beautiful picture of his unconditional love and mercy.

If God was able to use these women despite their pasts, just imagine how he will redeem *your* past and use your life for his good and perfect plan. If only you will let him.

• • •

You will be a crown of splendor in the LORD's hand,
a royal diadem in the hand of your God. (Isaiah 62:3)

My past can't be forgiven.

Women who believe this lie often say:
- God could never forget what I've done in the past.
- God is disappointed by my mistakes.
- Even though I know I'm forgiven, my actions still haunt me.
- I have so many regrets.
- My mistakes will keep God from blessing me in the future.

God will redeem your past and your mistakes.

God says:
- **Your sins are forgiven and forgotten.**
  He has removed our sins as far from us as the east is from the west. (Psalm 103:12, NLT)

- **I don't remember your sins.**
  For I will forgive their wickedness and will remember their sins no more. (Jeremiah 31:34b)

- **I forgive the guilt of your sin.**
  Then I acknowledged my sin to you and did not cover up my iniquity. I said, "I will confess my transgressions to the LORD." And you forgave the guilt of my sin. (Psalm 32:5)

- **I bring freedom and release from regrets.**
  He has sent me to bind up the brokenhearted, to proclaim freedom for the captives and release from darkness for the prisoners. (Isaiah 61:1b)

- **I will turn your ashes into beauty.**
  . . . to bestow on them a crown of beauty instead of ashes, the oil of joy instead of mourning, and a garment of praise instead of a spirit of despair. (Isaiah 61:3)

Lies I Believe:

....

....

....

....

....

....

....

....

....

Truth I Want to Remember:

....

....

....

....

....

....

....

....

....

Lie #5: I'm not beautiful.

I never really liked summer camp. I was a shy child and didn't make friends easily. When I was ten years old, I decided to be brave and spend a week at church camp during the summer. My little sister went with me. The first big setback came when my sister and I realized we had to stay in separate cabins across camp from each other. We were inseparable, so this was devastating news. We saw each other only once each day at the swimming pool. We clung to each other for those few precious minutes every day.

The second setback would carry a much deeper scar. One of the fun girls in my cabin befriended me. I was excited to have a friend, but our alliance was fleeting. One afternoon in crafts class, she looked at me and said, "You know, you're ugly. Well, I guess you aren't totally ugly, but your hair definitely is." I acted like it wasn't a big deal at all. I stuck my nose up in the air and walked away, ending our friendship. I didn't shed a tear because I didn't want her to know she hurt me.

Later that night in my (very uncomfortable) bunk bed, I pondered her statement. *Am I really ugly?* In my logical ten-year-old mind, I knew she wouldn't have said that if it weren't true. I absorbed the ugly lie right there, and it took many years to fully believe otherwise.

Back home a few months after summer camp, I had a very different experience. My best friend, Monica, had a slumber party to celebrate her birthday. Many of the popular girls from school were there, so I tried hard to fit in. I inwardly groaned when someone said, "Let's have a beauty pageant." Still raw from my camp friend's declaration, I prayed it would be over soon.

Unfortunately, sixth grade girls are serious about their beauty pageants, and the event lasted most of the evening and included various outfit changes and a talent segment. I numbly participated and had very low expectations when Monica's older sister and her best friend announced the final results.

When they chose me as the winner, I didn't have to fake shock like those beauty queens on television. I truly couldn't believe they picked me over my co-contestants, some of the prettiest girls from school. Now I realize I'm talking about a beauty pageant in my friend's basement. Nevertheless, even though it happened more than twenty-five years ago, I can still recall that moment as vividly as if I had been named Miss America on a Hollywood stage.

Although these two events in my childhood seem quite different on the surface, they're actually very similar. In both cases, I allowed my self-image to be based on external sources. I let my definition of beauty be set by others. When my friend called me ugly, I felt ugly. When my peers chose me as the winner in that pageant, I felt like the most beautiful girl in the world. And I haven't stopped there.

I feel beautiful when the man I'm dating thinks I'm beautiful. When a man is interested in me, the image in the mirror suddenly looks better to me. In reality, I'm not being as hard on myself as I normally am. Why does it take the attention of a man for me to be more respectful of that image in the mirror?

There are certainly women out there who don't struggle with physical beauty issues, but I meet far more women who do fight this battle. I have some very beautiful friends. I always assume they would never struggle with any type of self-image issues. Then, we start talking and sharing.

Isabel's Story

I accompanied my friend Isabel to her hometown in Texas. When I'm with Isabel, I usually feel like an ugly duckling. The truth is, it's not her fault. She's one of the kindest people I've ever met, and she's also one of the most beautiful people I know. Isabel's family is originally from Mexico, and she has gorgeous dark skin, hair, and eyes. While at brunch on our fun vacation, I almost choked on my huevos rancheros when she admitted to me that she often struggles with self-image issues.

Growing up in south Texas, Isabel came to believe the typical dark skin and features were ordinary and dull. She added, "I always admired the girls with fair skin, blonde hair, and blue eyes. To me, they were the distinctive and beautiful ones." My gorgeous friend grew up wishing she looked different. I did grow up with blonde hair and blue eyes, and I sat there wishing I looked like Isabel.

This is an area where Satan gets huge benefit from planting a few little lies. Lies we obsess over, lies we absorb very deep into our souls. And he laughs and laughs because we distract ourselves from God's truth for hours, days, and months as we sit and moan, "My legs are fat. My hair is ugly. Why can't I have a beautiful body like hers?"

The Comparison Game

One of the most destructive thought patterns occurs when I start comparing myself to others. I wish I had her stick-straight hair. I wish my skin were as clear as hers. Why can't I have cute clothes and good fashion sense like her? Comparing ourselves to others will spiral down into a pity party more quickly than just about anything else.

And it works with my single status too. Why can't I have a husband like hers who is so dedicated to his faith? I wish I had two adorable children just like hers. Why is she married while I'm still all alone?

The comparison game is a dangerous one that steals our contentment. When I'm not constantly comparing my life to others, I enjoy it. I travel a lot, hang out with a great group of close friends, and spend time on hobbies I enjoy. Yet when I focus on what I *don't* have instead of what I do, I become miserable. I feel alienated because it seems like I'm the last single girl left in Nashville. I feel discontent that I don't have a husband, child, and three-bedroom house with a nursery.

Facebook and other social media tools don't help the cause in this area. As we know, people like to show themselves in the very best light. We all pick and choose what we share on the Internet. But I tend to forget that truth when I start browsing the news feed and seeing everyone's ideal vacations, perfect husband, and adorable children. I feel like I'm the only one who struggles with contentment.

In my life, God used a Christian counselor to help me overcome some very deep-rooted lies about myself. Believe me, it wasn't fun or easy. It's much easier to keep believing the lies. Who wants to drag up all those old, painful memories? Even though I have dealt with many issues in the self-image area, I still struggle from time to time, just like most of my girlfriends.

The issue of self image is not exclusive to women either. When I surveyed a group of single men, an overwhelming 65 percent of them chose the statement, "I'm not attractive" as a lie they have believed about themselves. Of the ten myths in this book, this one ranked in first place as the answer most often chosen by single men respondents.

Thomas, 32, is a recently married friend of mine. When asked to describe one of the lies he believed during his single years, Thomas replied, "I have to change my physical appearance to find a girlfriend or wife. I need to work out and be muscular to attract women."

With the perspective of a newlywed looking back on his single years, Thomas said, "Looking back, God used every experience and heartache to mold and shape me into the man I needed to be, at the very moment I needed to be. It was so hard to trust him so many times, but he never left me alone. He was right there."

Rosalyn's Story

Any time she is around, my friend Rosalyn lights up the room. She is a fair-haired fireball with a passion for Jesus and all things southern. Even though she defines the term "extrovert" and I'm on the introverted side of the personality scale, our friendship works really well. Because confidence exudes from her five-foot-one frame, I was surprised to learn that negative self-image is something she battles.

> Everyone is different, and you have to become comfortable in your own skin. Truly start to love and appreciate who you are and embrace your singleness. Only then will you be ready to fully embrace the relationship you truly desire.
>
> —Robin, 31, single

"It began for me when I was eleven years old and hit puberty," Rosalyn confided. "My body began to change, and all of a sudden, I felt fat." At that time, Rosalyn was only a size three. Even though her intellect told her otherwise, her eyes saw a body that was developing curves and transforming. "My parents were going through a pretty rough divorce at that time. I turned to anorexia to cope. I starved myself because it was something I could control."

Looking back, Rosalyn sees how her negative body image and anorexia affected her actions and decisions. "I would avoid my friends' birthday parties because I didn't want to eat the cake, which had too many calories and fat grams." Rosalyn sadly added, "I was worried I might gain a pound."

Later, when she had mostly recovered from anorexia, Rosalyn's negative self-image still carried its consequences into her twenties and thirties. "This desire to feel beautiful caused me to date a couple of less-than-desirable guys. I felt intoxicated because they thought I was beautiful. So, I let them fill me up instead of the

Lord." She quickly realized this was an endless cycle. "It doesn't last long, and you need more and more of their flattery to fill you up."

Because of everything she has experienced, I asked Rosalyn for some advice in this area. How do we fight the lie telling us we're not beautiful? With her unique passion for life, Rosalyn replied, "I refuse to let Satan win, so I just continually keep asking Jesus to give me the eyes to see myself as he sees me. It doesn't happen overnight, and it requires discipline to spend time with him and focus on his Word, replacing the lies with his truth. Unlike the empty flattery from the men I have dated, his love is the spring that never runs dry."

God knows all of the things that have hurt you deeply. He knows the scars from words spoken—intentionally or unintentionally—by others. If you ask him for healing, he will do it. He loves to heal the wounds of his children. He may use a counselor, a friend, the Bible, or another method. He will show you the truth.

Truth: You are a beautiful woman made in God's image.

I know this is a tough one for many of us to absorb. I can almost read your mind. You're thinking, "She doesn't know me. How can she say I'm beautiful?"

In the book of Psalms, we find a scriptural basis for this: I praise you because I am fearfully and wonderfully made; your works are wonderful, I know that full well. My frame was not hidden from you when I was made in the secret place, when I was woven together in the depths of the earth. Your eyes saw my unformed body; all the days ordained for me were written in your book before one of them came to be. (Psalm 139:14-16)

That's how important you are to God. He created you exactly the way you are for a specific purpose. He wove you together. You are his masterpiece. He ordained all of your days before the earth was ever formed. God also knew the parts of yourself that would cause you sadness and struggle.

We can be very hard on ourselves. One of the things I'm learning is how to be gentle with myself. I say some really mean things. I look in the mirror and tell the reflection she looks fat. And pale. I bemoan my frizzy hair and splotchy skin. I would never say those kinds of things to a friend. So why do I say them to myself?

When I start thinking negative thoughts about myself, I have to immediately stop and refuse to allow those thoughts to completely form in my mind. I quote 2 Corinthians 10:5, which tells me to "take captive every thought" and "make it obedient to Christ."

Would Jesus want me thinking these negative thoughts about the person he lovingly created? No. So I stop and make the thought obedient to Christ. Sometimes, I have to do this multiple times each hour of each day. I do it until it becomes a habit to stop negative thought patterns.

> We say that beauty is in the eye of the beholder, but we often forget that our beholder is God.
>
> —Barbara, 38, single

Author Hudson Russell Davis says, "Anyone who sees themselves as ugly grants another person the power to determine the standard of beauty."[1] This is important for you as a single woman, because learning how to love yourself is the first step in the process of loving someone else the way God intended (and letting him love you back).

We need to eliminate the negative self-talk and talk to ourselves the way we speak to our friends. Let's try something. For one week, when you wake up each morning, I want you to look in the mirror and say, "God created me in his image. He designed me exactly right because he does not make mistakes. I am beautiful." Actually, I want you to say this to the mirror every day for the rest of your life. But start with one week and see how it feels. You really have nothing to lose.

God as Creator

We can go to the very beginning of the Bible to see God's character as our Creator. I love how it's stated twice in the same verse that we are created in the image of God. It's almost like God knew we would need the reminder: "So God created mankind in his own image, in the image of God he created them; male and female he created them" (Genesis 1:27).

I think we tend to take this for granted, especially since some of us have heard this passage our entire lives. The almighty God—the one whose goodness and love cannot adequately be described in words—created us *in his own image*. And then after he created us, he declared it was good: "God saw all that he had made, and it was very good" (Genesis 1:31a).

God says his creation is good. Who am I to question the one who designed me? Can you imagine a painting telling the artist that it would have preferred a little more red in the background?

We should ultimately be more concerned about inner beauty than our outward appearance. I'm not advocating we stop taking care of ourselves. Where do we draw the line? I know there are people who would call me vain for some of my choices. God created me with curly hair that I straighten and brown hair that I lighten. Each woman has a different outlook on enhancing her appearance and what is acceptable. However, the Bible is clear about the source of our beauty:

Your beauty should not come from outward adornment, such as elaborate hairstyles and the wearing of gold jewelry or fine clothes. Rather, it should be that of your inner self, the unfading beauty of a gentle and quiet spirit, which is of great worth in God's sight. (1 Peter 3:3-4)

This is a big struggle for single women. We think, "I want to be attractive so that my future husband is attracted to me." We have heard that men are more visual than women. It's important to have a nice appearance. But I also know that beauty fades, and I want him to be attracted to much more than the outward show.

The type of beauty that doesn't fade, the kind that is "of great worth in God's sight," will attract the type of man who is seeking the Lord. A widely known quote offers this advice: "A woman's heart should be so hidden in God that a man has to seek Him just to find her."[2] Although the source of the quotation is disputed, it's a good definition of a deeper kind of beauty.

Recently, a verse that's been on my mind is Matthew 6:21. In this verse, Jesus says, "For where your treasure is, there your heart will be also." If you looked at my checkbook some months, you might say that I treasure pedicures, hair treatments, and days at the spa. I need to be careful that my heart doesn't get stuck tending to my vanity.

God delights in us and rejoices over us (see Isaiah 62:4-5). Ultimately, our sense of beauty needs to come from our Creator. Our confidence needs to come from him instead of our outward appearance. We need to be concerned about building inner beauty, tending to our spirits as much as our bodies. Unlike my body, my spirit is eternal.

My friend Rosalyn now understands this. She muses, "When do you feel God's love the most? Really ponder that and then let God indulge you with those moments. He created these passions in you, so let him show you, through them, just how beautiful you are."

A Beautiful Thing

I searched the words of Jesus in the Bible to see if he used the word "beautiful." I only found one instance, and I think it carries a message for us.

It's the story about the woman who interrupted a dinner party. Jesus was dining at the home of Simon the leper. A woman who wasn't invited to the party approached Jesus as he reclined at the table. She took out a jar of very expensive perfume and poured it on his head. (See Matthew 26:7; Matthew and Mark both describe the woman pouring the perfume on Jesus' head while dining at the home of Simon the leper, but the gospel of John describes a similar story of Mary pouring perfume on Jesus' feet.)

Have you ever experienced God asking you to do something that felt uncomfortable? You knew what he wanted you to do, but it took a big leap of faith to actually step out and obey. I wonder if this woman felt the same way. I'm sure she was devoted to Jesus, and her love made her task easier. But it's pretty unnerving to crash a dinner party and pour out perfume on someone's head, even back in that day.

Jesus' followers weren't pleased at all. The disciples called her action a waste and mumbled that the perfume could have been sold for money to give to the poor. Jesus, aware of their discontent, said, "Why are you bothering this woman? She has done a *beautiful* thing to me" (Matthew 26:10, emphasis mine).

"Beautiful" is a strong word. The Greek word used here (*kalon*) didn't just have moral implications. It also had a visual component. Jesus declared this woman's obedient action to be beautiful. He basically called her beautiful. Can you imagine how she felt?

She poured herself out for him with an offering of expensive perfume. She may have spent all of her money on that little jar. She gave him everything, and he called it beautiful.

That's the kind of beauty I want to achieve. The kind of beauty that doesn't fade. The kind that's not based on what a man thinks of me or how pretty my friends believe I am. I want to attain beauty by fulfilling my purpose and by pouring myself out in obedience to God.

• • •

The king is enthralled by your beauty. (Psalm 45:11, 1984 NIV)

The Lie

I'm not beautiful.

Women who believe this lie often say:

- I wish I were _____ (thinner, prettier, shorter, taller . . .).
- I don't like my _____ (thighs, hair, skin, feet, nose . . .).
- I would have a husband if I were more beautiful.
- I need to lose weight to be attractive.
- I don't leave my house without makeup applied and hair styled.

The Truth

You are a beautiful woman made in God's image.

God says:

- **I am enthralled with you.**
  The king is enthralled by your beauty. (Psalm 45:11, 1984 NIV)
- **I created you in my image.**
  So God created mankind in his own image, in the image of God he created them; male and female he created them. (Genesis 1:27)
- **My creation is perfect and good.**
  God saw all that he had made, and it was very good. (Genesis 1:31a)
- **I don't make mistakes.**
  All the days ordained for me were written in your book before one of them came to be. (Psalm 139:16)
- **Your beauty comes from within.**
  Your beauty should not come from outward adornment, such as elaborate hairstyles and the wearing of gold jewelry or fine clothes. Rather, it should be that of your inner self, the unfading beauty of a gentle and quiet spirit, which is of great worth in God's sight. (1 Peter 3:3-4)

Lies I Believe:

....

....

....

....

....

....

....

....

....

Truth I Want to Remember:

....

....

....

....

....

....

....

....

....

Lie #6: Getting married will solve all my problems.

For many of us who have never been married, we pin many expectations, dreams, and hopes on marriage. Since I was a little girl, I have been dreaming about my fairy-tale husband. As I get older, I just add more expectations to the list. He'll know what I need from him without me having to say a word. He won't have any bad habits and will never annoy me. He'll always be confident (but never arrogant). Oh yeah, he'll also be a great cook, clean up after himself, and basically solve all my problems. Of course, I can hear the laughter of all my married friends echoing in my head. I know this picture isn't realistic. But the longer I stay single, the more expectations I attach to this imaginary husband.

I get so tired of doing life alone. God has placed amazing friends in my life. I definitely don't live in isolation, sulking and waiting for a spouse. Although I live in community with others, I watch married couples and become envious of their partnership. Many of the couples I know talk things over and share ideas with each other. They cook dinner together and do home repair projects as a team. They have a built-in date to work functions and weddings. These couples go on vacation together and share meals with each other. Basically, they do life together.

Brooke is twenty-five and single. Sometimes, she believes marriage would eliminate her loneliness and make life a little easier. "When I'm stressed taking care of my car, home repairs, or finances, I can't help but think it would be so much easier with a man's help." She also believes marriage would satisfy her desire to be truly known and loved. Brooke says that being married would make a statement to the world: "I'm important enough, pretty enough, and interesting enough for someone to want to be with me." She would no longer have to worry about whether someone could love her.

My friend Kristi also tells me her image of marriage is one of being known and loved. "I know marriage won't fix loneliness, but it fixes aloneness, which goes a long way toward decreasing the lonely factor."

Brooke and Kristi both make valid points. We all desire to be known and loved. We know marriage brings many challenges and no marriage is perfect. But most of us want the opportunity to share our lives with a spouse. We know the spousal relationship will likely be the most intimate and intense relationship we will have in this world. Getting married will fulfill many of our desires. And honestly, it does solve a few of those things we view as problems.

The trouble arises when we start believing the lie that someone other than God will satisfy our deep longings. When we heap all our hopes, dreams, and longings on a spouse, it creates a recipe for hurt feelings and dashed expectations. No man on this earth can meet those needs. If he doesn't run away in fear, he will be exhausted and still feel like he's not measuring up.

> Single or married, with kids or without, we are all sinners. We all have issues to deal with. Just because you are single, it doesn't necessarily mean that your issues are more significant. Believing the lie and living your life as if that is true won't get you anywhere; it will only lead to confusion.
> —Kristi, 33, single

Marriage—a Problem Solver?

I interviewed Brooke, Kristi, and a number of other women, both single and married, regarding the topic of marriage and whether it can solve problems faced by singles. Their answers were quite insightful, and I want to share some of them with you.

The following quotes were in response to my question, "What advice would you share with single women who believe getting married would help solve their problems?"

• • •

Whatever problems you have before you're married will carry over into your marriage. Being married might solve some of your problems, but it creates new problems. There are many good things that come with marriage, but it also comes with its own dose of hardships and difficulties.

—Brooke, 25, single

• • •

Marriage doesn't solve problems. You need to be secure and know who you are in the Lord before joining in a life with someone. I have learned to enjoy the journey. It may not be the plan we have for our own lives, but the Lord knows what is best. He is always preparing us for what's next. If we just sit and yearn for marriage, we may miss the lesson we're supposed to be learning now.

—Danielle, 31, single

• • •

God works on our hearts as individuals, so having a spouse or significant other doesn't necessarily fix those kinds of problems. It might actually enhance them. Let God deal with your heart and emotions right now, and don't wait for a spouse to come along before dealing with those issues.

—Liz, 31, single

• • •

Surrounded by a culture that believes in fairy-tale romances and happy endings where everyone has a Prince Charming, it's easy to get carried away and set ourselves up for disappointment. If we could see the beauty in each moment of our lives and be content with that, we would discover a much more fulfilling and true life than could be found in any movie.

—*Anne, 28, married*

• • •

There are advantages to being single and only having to worry about you. When you're married, sometimes you can't make a decision solely based on your wants, thoughts, or needs because there is another person involved. Every stage of life has problems. The challenge is to see them as opportunities to learn and grow, to pray through them, and see what God wants you to know.

—*Catherine, 45, married*

• • •

Even as a wife, I still find it so vital to bask in the Father's true love. Whereas I know my husband loves me, I still need to learn to bask in God's unfailing love.

—*Andrea, 34, married*

• • •

I realize everyone has a different view and handles singleness in her own way. A close friend of mine, Samantha, is thirty-five and has never been married. She is wise and introspective, and her story may resonate with you. Samantha told me:

I'm thankful for the perspective on marriage being an "older" single has given me. I readily admit I had the "prince on a white horse/love at first sight/live happily ever after" view of marriage. After seeing friends marry, divorce, and remarry and hearing stories about the day-to-day struggles of marriage over the years, all of it has sobered me. Most of my friends were in it for the "ever after" part, but the "happily" part seemed to be missing.

At times, I wonder if I might be better off single. I think it's easier. There's no conflict resolution to deal with on a potentially daily basis. I don't have to work around anyone else's schedule, and my time is truly mine. No compromise is necessary, no financial accountability required. There's no need to risk vulnerability.

Samantha acknowledges certain disadvantages to the single life as well. "I remember being angry at God for my singleness when I had to get rid of mice in the mouse traps! I so wanted a godly man at that moment."

Lest I leave you with the image of Samantha emptying the mouse traps alone for the rest of her life, she has realized that marriage—though not a problem solver and potentially a problem creator—may be the tool God uses in her life to refine her. "God made us to be in relationships. They will be messy and difficult, but that's where he meets us, molds us, and makes us into the person we were fully intended to be."

A Woman with a Past

We meet a woman in the Bible who seems to have plenty of problems. We don't know if she pinned her hopes and dreams on a spouse, but we do know she experienced a lot of failed relationships. So many, in fact, that she was most likely an outcast in her community. Her story reminds me of a familiar quote by Laurel Thatcher Ulrich that says, "Well-behaved women sel-

> Take a break! Focusing on the idea of marriage and all that relates to it can be exhausting. I've spent so much time trying to bolster myself as a strong, grounded, healthy Christian woman in order to be attractive and ready for marriage. Once I knew I was taking all the outward actions to be social and meet people in the right places, I started focusing on myself. I strongly suggest counseling as an avenue for God's healing touch, but I don't think we should stress about the idea of being fully "fixed" or in a good enough place personally to ever be able to marry. God's got the timing!
>
> —Alexis, 29, single

dom make history."[1] In the case of this particular historical account, it seems to be true.

I'm talking about the story in the fourth chapter of John where Jesus encountered a woman at a well in Samaria. The woman visited the well at noon, the hottest part of the day, to draw water. Many commentators acknowledge this fact to imply she was an outcast among the other women in the village. She wasn't included in the group of women who came together to socialize and draw water early in the morning or later in the afternoon.

Since the woman was a Samaritan, she was quite shocked when Jesus asked her for a drink of water. She would have known by his clothes and dialect that he was Jewish. A Jew would not drink from a Samaritan's water jar. In fact, the Samaritans were despised by most Jews. John Piper explains the situation and background well:

> We have ethnic, racial, and religious issues here that made Jews feel disdain for Samaritans. They were ceremonially unclean. They were racially impure. They were religiously heretical. And therefore they were avoided.[2]

Jesus, of course, didn't allow any of those factors to stop him from a divine encounter with this woman. Samaritan or Jewish, woman or man, a handful of "little" sins or a lifetime of "big" ones—none of it changes God's love for his children.

As they dialogued about the living water he could provide her, Jesus asked the woman to go and return with her husband. She was honest with him by saying she didn't have a husband. The next words Jesus spoke could easily be misinterpreted: "Jesus said to her, 'You are right when you say you have no husband. The fact is, you have had five husbands, and the man you now have is not your husband. What you have just said is quite true'" (John 4:17b-18).

He didn't say those words with condemnation. He said them with love. How do I know that? I know because God is compassionate and loving. From personal experience, I know he doesn't speak in a condemning voice. Second, I know it's true because of the woman's response. She doesn't get angry, run away, or become defensive. She acknowledges the truth of his statement by calling him a prophet.

She feels safe with Jesus. She's still trying to figure out who he is, but I believe she understands one thing. She is fully known, and at the same time, fully loved and accepted by this man. Do those words sound familiar? To be fully known and loved is what each of us desires.

> *Truth: Only God can satisfy our deep longings to be fully known and loved.*

A spouse won't save us from our problems. Only a life-changing interaction with Jesus will bring peace into our lives. Marriage is a good thing that may solve some of our problems. But it won't save us.

God as Savior

After this prolonged time of being single, I have begun to feel like I deserve things. I deserve a loving husband and beautiful, well-behaved children. I start to get angry with God because I believe he owes me these things. I have expectations, and he is not meeting them.

I forget each breath I take is because God allows it to happen. I overlook the fact that every moment is a blessing. I don't remember to be grateful for all the things I've been given. I neglect to remember that God is and has always been. That he is the one worthy of all my praise.

When I get angry because my desires aren't being fulfilled, I fail to understand his holiness. I don't recall that what I truly deserve—because of my sins—is death. Romans 6:23 tells me death is the penalty for my sin. Thankfully, it goes on to say that I have a gift of eternal life through Jesus.

When I was in elementary and junior high school, I brought my lunch to school. My mom would often include little handwritten notes along with my lunch. Although I pretended like they weren't a big deal, those notes meant the world to me. I still remember that feeling of being completely loved and knowing I truly belonged to someone.

For so long, my single status held power over me. Being alone, I felt disappointment and emptiness. I'm grateful that God is allowing me to begin to understand a small portion of his love. Because I'm unconditionally loved by him, I can celebrate love and share that love with others around me.

It took me a very long time to realize God's love and acceptance is the only thing that would fill the void in my heart. I chased romantic love, believing I would be complete when someone loved me back. I chased success, believing my value would finally be established with a high-ranking job title. God patiently waited for me to finally understand that he created me to crave his unconditional love.

My mother's love was something God used to prepare me to comprehend the greatness of his love. But God is the one who wrote the ultimate love story. He sent Jesus to be our true Savior. God loves us so much that he sent his Son to suffer and die so we can be reconciled to him. "But God demonstrates his own love for us in this: While we were still sinners, Christ died for us" (Romans 5:8). That is amazing love. God's love is the only kind of love that's everlasting. He is the only one who will fulfill the deepest desires of our hearts. He created us that way—with a longing for him.

We try to satisfy our longings with so many other things. For a while, those things may work. Ultimately, though, we have to turn back to the author of our story.

Leave Your Water Jar Behind

Jesus shared his ultimate love story with the woman at the well. He shared his identity with her, and she believed. I can't help but think it's what she had been seeking all along. "The woman said, 'I know that Messiah' (called Christ) 'is coming. When he comes, he will explain everything to us.' Then Jesus declared, 'I, the one speaking to you—I am he'" (John 4:25-26).

After her encounter with Jesus, the Samaritan woman was so changed that she went to tell others about Jesus: "Then, leaving her water jar, the woman went back to the town and said to the people, 'Come, see a man who told me everything I ever did. Could this be the Messiah?' They came out of the town and made their way toward him" (John 4:28-30).

Why does the Bible tell us she left her water jar behind? I don't know for sure, but I think every detail is important in Scripture. I believe it gives us an image. When we have a life-changing encounter with the God of the universe, we often find ourselves leaving behind the things we were grasping onto so tightly.

Personally, I need to leave behind the growing list of expectations I have for my future husband. Instead of focusing on the list of qualities I want in a husband, I need to focus on my own journey and purpose in God's eyes. In order to be the woman God designed me to become, I must leave behind my water jar full of expectations. Instead, I choose to accept God's living water, which is what I need to grow and flourish.

I challenge you to figure out what's in your water jar. Leave it behind. Empty out your expectations, hopes, and dreams. Leave them with God—they are in good hands. I'm not saying you should completely give up your hopes and dreams. Hold them loosely while trusting in the Lord. Delight in him, the only one who can satisfy. Accept his water and let your spirit flourish and grow with him.

● ● ●

Trust in the LORD and do good; dwell in the land and enjoy safe pasture. Take delight in the LORD, and he will give you the desires of your heart. (Psalm 37:3-4)

Getting married will solve all my problems.

Women who believe this lie often say:
- Marriage will cure my loneliness.
- A spouse will fulfill all my longings.
- I will feel completely beautiful, loved, and known once I'm married.
- A husband's love will eliminate my insecurities and keep me safe.
- Marriage will save me from my sadness.

Only God can satisfy our deep longings to be fully known and loved.

God says:

- **When you're lonely, seek me with all your heart.**
  You will seek me and find me when you seek me with all your heart. (Jeremiah 29:13)

- **I am the husband who will fulfill your deepest longings.**
  For your Maker is your husband—the LORD Almighty is his name—the Holy One of Israel is your Redeemer. (Isaiah 54:5)

- **My love is the only everlasting and complete love.**
  I have loved you with an everlasting love; I have drawn you with unfailing kindness. (Jeremiah 31:3)

- **Take refuge in me, and I will keep your way secure.**
  As for God, his way is perfect: The LORD's word is flawless; he shields all who take refuge in him. . . . It is God who arms me with strength and keeps my way secure. (Psalm 18:30-32)

- **I am your Savior. Put your hope in me.**
  Guide me in your truth and teach me, for you are God my Savior, and my hope is in you all day long. (Psalm 25:5)

Lies I Believe:

....
....
....
....
....
....
....
....
....

Truth I Want to Remember:

....
....
....
....
....
....
....
....
....
....

Lie #7: There is something wrong with me.

While walking my dog in the neighborhood, I ran into a former colleague who had been my supervisor at a previous job. I heard he and his spouse had moved back to town, but we hadn't seen each other in about seven years. Excited to see him, I stopped to chat. The first words out of his mouth were, "Are you married?" Seriously, those were the very first words he spoke, without even a "Hello!" or "How are you?" Shocked, I replied with a simple no. The immediate follow-up question was similar. "Are you engaged?" Again answering in the negative form, I quickly shifted the conversation to focus on him.

Those were the only two questions he asked me throughout the conversation. He didn't ask where I was working or whether I kept up with our friends from the previous job. He didn't want to know if I still traveled a lot or enjoyed my condominium in the neighborhood. I felt ashamed and embarrassed that I couldn't produce more exciting or romantic news to share with him.

For just a moment, I considered making up a story to share. "No, I'm not married or engaged, but I met the man of my dreams a few months ago. He's arriving in a few minutes, and we're going to look at engagement rings." Or something along those lines. Instead, I walked away feeling like something was wrong with me. What have I been doing for the past seven years since I last saw my coworker? His eyes seemed to ask that exact question after each of my negative responses.

At age thirty-six, I started referring to myself as an "old maid" when people asked about my marital status. Honestly, I don't see myself that way, but I guess it's my defense mechanism. I say it with a chuckle before the other person can think it. Our society isn't quite sure what to do with a woman in her mid-thirties who has never been married. Most small talk revolves around spouses and families. I get strange looks when I vacation or dine alone. Since I have a rather introverted personality, I honestly don't mind doing either, but the reactions of other people sometimes make me feel uncomfortable.

Sarah, a single woman in her mid-thirties, shared a story that made a huge impact on me. "A friend of mine lost her right leg in the Haiti earthquake. When I was with her a few weeks ago, I had an odd realization. I feel like a one-legged person in a two-legged world. It feels as if there is something clearly wrong with me. Everyone can see I don't have a partner."[1]

As a single person in a world full of married people, we can feel isolated and different. I've found it's more socially acceptable to be in your late thirties and divorced than the same age and never married. Elayne Boosler, comedian and writer, once said, "I've never been married, but I tell people I'm divorced so they won't think something's wrong with me."[2]

This particular lie is another one that isn't gender specific. In my survey, 55 percent of the men said they have believed something is wrong with them due to their single status. I asked some of my male friends to describe how it feels to be over thirty years old and single. Jake, who is thirty-six, said. "I have been in ten of my friends' weddings. I'm genuinely happy for them. That being said, it made single awareness more real as years passed and relationships with girls ended. All the while, my close friends' lives seemed to progress with things that are important to me, such as having a loving spouse and children."

Jake admits this takes a toll on him. "As a result of this reality and relationships not working out, I struggle with thoughts of 'what is wrong with me?' or 'why do I keep choosing these types of girls?' I've also struggled with no longer fitting into the lives of my married friends. Although we're still close friends, I seem to make new friends who are single and spend time with them."

James is another friend who is now married but recalls the discouragement of his single years. "Numerous times, I thought there was something wrong with me because I was thirty and unmarried. My family and friends would always encourage me and tell me what a catch I would be for some girl, but apparently no girls thought that. It was discouraging to me." James is now married to a beautiful, godly woman and they have three children with one more on the way!

> We need to speak truth to ourselves. We might feel like something is wrong with us or that God is withholding good things from us. Just because we feel that way doesn't necessarily mean that it's reality.
>
> —Brooke, 25, single

"You're so pretty. I can't believe you're not married." I actually hear that a lot these days, and the comment always baffles me. I know the remark is made with good intentions. In a backwards way, it's a compliment. But the logic doesn't work. I'm fairly confident being pretty or beautiful isn't a qualification for marriage. We know beauty takes various forms and is subjective. In another subtle way, comments like these endorse the belief that there must be something wrong with the person who has never married. When people say this to me, I imagine their inner monologue to be: "Well, she's pretty, so that's not the reason she is single. There must be something else then."

Brooke, the twenty-five-year-old single woman whom you met in a previous chapter, also struggles with this. She often hears the question, "How is a great girl like you still single?" She says, "It's meant to be a type of compliment, but it doesn't help." Unfortunately, she's also had some negative experiences with Christian men who pursued her and then said she wasn't what they were looking for in a wife. Brooke said, "It definitely made me feel as if there was something wrong with me—something causing me to be single still."

Annie, who is thirty-three and married, admitted to me that she sometimes has to stop and realign her thinking. "I've had to repent for thinking things such as, 'I wonder why she isn't married. She is totally marriage material.' Who are we to say that? As Christians, we try to play the role of God a lot."

At age fifty-four, Julie has never married. She is tired of explaining that fact. When she goes on dates, her date often starts the conversation by asking, "Why have you never been married?" Julie admits, "I have always wanted to be married, so I truly believe there is something wrong with me because I haven't been able to make it work out, even though I've been successful in my career and my friendships."

I could keep going. These are only a few of the many responses I heard from single women about this topic. It breaks my heart because this lie is one that's so easy to believe. We are frequently our harshest critics. That reality, combined with the pressure today's culture places on young women to find a husband, can make any woman over the age of thirty—or even twenty-five in some cases—feel desperate and alone.

This pressure can lead to bad decisions. I'll talk more about settling for less than God's best in another chapter, but believing the lie that something is wrong with us can cause us to settle instead of waiting for God's plan to work out.

Ruth's Journey

If you've grown up in church like me, you'll be tempted to skim through this section since Ruth's story is familiar. I hope you won't, though, because I'm taking a different approach to the typical commentary. I promise I'm not going to tell you how to find your Boaz in ten easy steps. In my opinion, that topic has been thoroughly covered by other authors and commentators.

I want to focus on the relationship between Ruth and God and the ways Ruth handled a difficult situation. If anyone had reason to believe something was wrong with her, it was Ruth. Ruth was a widow. I'm not saying that fact was her fault. As much as we sometimes believe it, our singleness is not our fault either. If you look at Ruth's situation, though, it was pretty bleak.

Ruth, a woman from Moab, married into a Judean family. That fact alone probably didn't go over well with her family of origin. Within the first ten years of her marriage, her father-in-law, brother-in-law, and husband all died. She was a young widow, surrounded by sadness. Additionally, her extended family had no male protector left for them in Moab. At this point, I imagine she may have questioned some of her decisions and probably wondered why her story was playing out in this manner.

In the Bible, the book of Ruth tells us that Ruth's mother-in-law, Naomi, became bitter about her circumstances and made a plan to return to Bethlehem, her homeland. At this point in her story, Ruth faced many choices. Like Naomi, she could have chosen the path of bitterness. She could have been satisfied looking over her shoulder, focusing on regrets, and choosing the path of the past. Naomi even tried to convince Ruth to return to her own family in Moab and find another husband. It may have been the easier path for her.

Yet Ruth shows us a little about her character when she makes her choice and speaks some of the most familiar words in the Bible (to Naomi):

> But Ruth replied, "Don't urge me to leave you or to turn back from you. Where you go I will go, and where you stay I will stay. Your people will be my people and your God my God. Where you die I will die, and there I will be buried. May the LORD

deal with me, be it ever so severely, if even death separates you and me." (Ruth 1:16-17)

I recently heard Liz Curtis Higgs speak about the book of Ruth, and she noted that God never actually speaks throughout the entire book, but he is seen all through it.[3] I believe God had been drawing Ruth to him and toward this very moment when she boldly declared her loyalty to Naomi and Naomi's God.

We can see God's hand throughout Ruth's story. I'm sure there were times she couldn't see it, though. In those times, she had to walk forward on faith alone. When I read through this book, I'm amazed by the moments God equips Ruth with courage, determination, and obedience.

In a foreign land, she was courageous to go alone into the fields and pick up leftover grain (see Ruth 2:3). Her determination shows in her work ethic and dedication to feed her family (see Ruth 2:17-18). Her obedience is evident when she listens to Naomi's wild request to go to the threshing floor and lie at Boaz's feet, something that would not have been an acceptable move for a single woman to make (see Ruth 3:3-6).

Ruth didn't try to manipulate or control her circumstances. She trusted God, and he led her to the field owned by Boaz. As a foreigner from another country, she held her head high and refused to believe something was wrong with her. She wasn't looking for a husband. She worked hard and provided food for her family. In the midst of difficult circumstances, Ruth showed loyalty to Naomi, faith in God's plan, and enormous courage.

Is it possible that God will also provide the same courage, determination, and faith for your specific journey? Is it feasible that there's really nothing wrong with you, but instead, that God has placed you in this place for a purpose, one that only you can accomplish?

> *Truth: You have been made by God for a purpose. Your loving Father will equip you with everything you need along the way.*

Mile Ten

A couple of years ago, I trained to run a half marathon. It was a huge undertaking because I had never run more than one full mile in my life before this training program. I now agree with the claims that distance running is a mental challenge as much as a physical one. The days I set out to run three miles, I can run *just* three. The days I set out to run eight miles, when I get to that three-mile mark, my mind knows I still have five more to go. So, I won't allow myself to get tired. I have to mentally prepare to run that next five miles.

Although I'm a very slow runner, I worked hard over the course of four months and slowly built up to running eight miles on weekends. But I knew eight wasn't going to be enough. On a spring morning, about a month before race day, I set out to run ten miles for the first time. On the popular five-mile trail (which I ran twice), I passed people pushing strollers, walking dogs, running, and biking. As I passed them, my neighbors didn't know whether I was on mile two or mile ten. Honestly, my external appearance was basically the same at both points. I didn't feel the same on the inside. By mile ten, I was fairly miserable and hurting badly. I wanted it to be over. But from the viewpoint of a passerby, I could have been just starting mile two.

Appearances are deceiving. When we encounter people in life, we don't know if they're running mile two, mile ten, or somewhere in between. It's the same for us. We don't know how much longer we'll be required to remain in the waiting room of singleness. We don't know the length of the course or how much longer our shoes need to hit the pavement. Based on outward appearances, it's difficult to know the number of miles logged—the number of years spent waiting, the number of pleas made to God, or the weight of the burdens carried.

Each one of us will run a unique race. Even before we were born, God knew the challenges we would encounter and the specific struggles we would face. Hebrews 12:1*b* reads, "And let us run with perseverance the race marked out for us."

Thankfully, we don't have to finish the course alone. The next verse, Hebrews 12:2 reads, "Fixing our eyes on Jesus, the pioneer and perfecter of faith. For the joy set before him he endured the cross, scorning its shame, and sat down at the right hand of the throne of God."

There is someone who understands our struggles and faced quite a few of his own. For his entire life, Jesus knew "mile ten" was coming. He lived each day knowing that death on a cross was his destiny. He would be despised, mocked, and scorned. Jesus lived as a human—knowing he would sacrifice his life for us.

When I struggle to continue running the race, I try to keep my eyes on Jesus. In the face of unimaginable circumstances, he remained obedient to God. Even while enduring a shameful death, he finished the course his Father set for him. Let's do the same. Run your specific race with faith in God—no matter how much it hurts or how long it ends up being—and meet him at the finish line.

> There is nothing wrong with you. . . . Live life to its fullest, surround yourself with people who love Jesus with all their hearts, and strive to trust. God has a wonderful hope and a future for you, just like he says.
>
> —Galina, 29, single

God as Abba Father

As our Father, God wants the best for us. Parents don't give their children everything they want the moment they want it. They have more wisdom and an understanding of what the child actually needs. Although I often see marriage as a need in my life, God is providing for my true needs in each moment. He's a loving Father, not a scary deity up in the sky withholding blessings from me. Brooke communicates this very well:

Ultimately, God is still sovereign and sees our hurt. Even if we don't fully understand or trust what God is doing, we need to trust his heart—trust that he truly loves us and doesn't see us as less important. We need to speak truth to ourselves. We might feel like something is wrong with us or that God is withholding good things from us, but just because we feel that way doesn't necessarily mean that's reality.

—*Brooke, 25, single*

• • •

Sometimes, I struggle to mesh the images of a holy, sovereign God with one I can call Daddy or Abba, a term of familiarity for fathers in Aramaic. In Romans, Paul uses this intimate expression and tells us to claim God as our Father.

For those who are led by the Spirit of God are the children of God. The Spirit you received does not make you slaves, so that you live in fear again; rather, the Spirit you received brought about your adoption to sonship. And by him we cry, "*Abba*, Father." The Spirit himself testifies with our spirit that we are God's children. (Romans 8:14-16)

I like this image of God as my adoptive Father. The times when I'm experiencing intimate relationship with God are the same times I'm less focused on my single status. I am better able to live in the present moment, not worried about the future. I can focus on my conversation with God. At these times, I completely understand the view of Brother Lawrence, who said, "There is not in the world a kind of life more sweet and delightful, than that of a continual conversation with God."[4]

My prayer is that each of you will enjoy freedom in the knowledge that God loves you like a Father. I pray you find peace in surrendering control back to him. Realize you're on a journey that's been hand-selected for you by your Father God. Lean into him and ask for guidance regarding the next steps. Ask him to give you what you need, according to his definition of necessity. Continue to run the race with faithfulness. And remember—there is nothing wrong with you.

• • •

I have fought the good fight, I have finished the race,
I have kept the faith. (2 Timothy 4:7)

The Lie

There is something wrong with me.

Women who believe this lie often say:

- God must not believe I will be a good wife.
- There is something I need to fix about myself before getting married.
- I'm still single because of mistakes I've made in the past.
- God doesn't understand my needs.
- I must not be good enough, pretty enough, _____ enough to be married.

The Truth

You have been made by God for a purpose. Your loving Father will equip you with everything you need along the way.

God says:

- **My power is best displayed in your weakness.**
  But he said to me, "My grace is sufficient for you, for my power is made perfect in weakness." Therefore I will boast all the more gladly about my weaknesses, so that Christ's power may rest on me. (2 Corinthians 12:9)

- **If you love me, all things work together for my purpose.**
  And we know that in all things God works for the good of those who love him, who have been called according to his purpose. (Romans 8:28)

- **I will meet all your needs.**
  And my God will meet all your needs according to the riches of his glory in Christ Jesus. (Philippians 4:19)

- **Come as you are. Rest in me.**
  Come to me, all you who are weary and burdened, and I will give you rest. (Matthew 11:28)

Lies I Believe:

....
....
....
....
....
....
....
....
....

Truth I Want to Remember:

....
....
....
....
....
....
....
....
....

Lie #8: The church values married people more than me.

Walking into the auditorium for Sunday morning church services, I dread the lonely feeling that will soon deposit itself in my stomach. Families are sitting together in their normal spots, chatting and getting ready for the service. With many familiar faces in the crowd, I could easily grab a seat and squeeze in next to one of my favorite families. I've done that before. But no matter how hard they try to make me feel welcome on their row, I still feel like an outsider.

Instead, I grab a seat in an empty row toward the back and open the bulletin. Sighing, I almost get up and walk out. The sermon is about marriage. Again. Instead of leaving, I push play on the self-lectures in my head. "It's good for you to learn about marriage now. You'll be an expert by the time you finally get married." I tell myself that my single status doesn't have to make me feel like a second-class citizen.

After being very involved in churches over the past decade as a single woman, it's easy to believe that today's churches are designed for families and cater only to married couples. Just reading the bulletin announcements, I see family movie nights and mothers' day out activities. These are all good things, things that aren't designed to make me feel like an outsider. Yet they do. I realize I don't have to be part of a couple or a family to be involved in church. I know they aren't trying to exclude or label me. Yet somehow, I still feel like the church values married people more than me.

I interviewed more than twenty single women about this topic to determine whether my feelings and experiences were unique or if other single women also struggled in church.

Laura is a twenty-seven-year-old single woman who attends church regularly. I asked if she had any experiences in a church setting where she felt less important than married women or families. "I wouldn't say I feel less important, but I do feel isolated," Laura notes. "One church I attended had lots of community groups for married couples but just one for singles." She also admits to feeling misunderstood at times. "If you don't have the same dream of having a husband, two kids, a dog, and a white picket fence, then you aren't really understood by a lot of church members."

Many women expressed concerns that their churches should be doing more to reach out to single members. Laura speculated, "It seems like for every ten sermons on marriage or parenting, there might be one on dealing with single life." Suzanne is a committed and valuable member of her church in Nashville. She remarks, "From the pulpit, marriage is definitely talked about proportionately more than it should be. The topics of singleness and relationship issues need to be discussed from the pulpit as well because there are probably as many divorced people, or couples struggling with conflict, as there are single people at my church."

This is a hard topic to address without sounding bitter about church. I don't think the church or its people intentionally try to make single people feel left out or different. It's much easier for churches to develop programs for children and families. Developing a dynamic singles ministry is difficult and has an attached stigma. Many churches try to include singles and develop a community for their unmarried members. In my experience, the result is either a group that people attend just to find someone to date, or it seems forced because marital status is the only thing these individuals have in common. The programs often fall flat, and when the group leaders get married, no one else steps up to carry on the leadership.

My friend Jordan had a more positive experience with her church family. "My church is great about pointing out the fruits of being single. The ladies in my church reach out to me just as much as their married counterparts." She admits to being aware of her singleness at church, but she places no blame on God or the church. "As a thirty-one-year-old single woman, I think my own insecurities make me feel odd at church sometimes." Jordan explains, "I see husbands and wives hold each other closely when hearing God's Word or praying. I can't help but want that. Resentment sometimes creeps up, but I know it is not of God."

I can identify with Jordan's insecurities. After getting fed up with church singles' groups, I started volunteering in the children's ministry at our church. I needed a way to get connected, meet people, and build relationships. Plus, I've always been pretty good with kids. But my work with the children's ministry seemed to further emphasize my single status in my mind. All of the parents dropping off their children to class were my age or younger. My clock was ticking, and I felt like I had a stamp on my forehead labeling me as the lonely single girl who teaches other people's children.

We tend to assign people to categories. And we're just not sure what to do with the unmarried crowd in our churches. Should we try to play matchmaker and set them up on dates with each other? Or, maybe this person is happy being single at this time in her life? I agree that it's difficult to know how to approach single women within the church. Many of my married church friends completely avoid the issue when talking to me. They don't want me to feel labeled or different. Some days, that works out well for me. On other days, I want my friends to introduce me to single, Christian men. How else am I going to meet my future husband?

Do we ignore labels altogether and treat everyone the same, or should we try to match up all the unmarried men and women in the church? I believe honesty is the key. It's important to be yourself and be real. If you're in the mood to be matched up, tell your married girlfriends at church. Don't be desperate, but let them know you're in a place where you would like to meet some nice, single men.

My desire is to see a community of people who love Jesus more than labels. I want to see married people inviting single friends over for dinner with their families. As a single woman, I need to invite families to my home for dinner. I want to be the person who reaches out to a single mother and welcomes her and her daughter to my table. We need to see the reality of each other's lives, not remain cloistered within our circles of friends with similar marital status. I dream of a church community that loves each other well, regardless of marital status or any other labels.

On his WAY-FM radio program, *Mornings with Brant*, Brant Hansen once said, "Church culture may be tilted toward married people. But that is not Christianity. Paul said being single is preferable. That was stunning at the time—totally countercultural at the time too."[1]

I agree with Brant that today's church culture seems slanted toward couples and families. Sometimes, singleness feels like a curse we need to overcome. How have we moved from singleness being a preferable state in the Bible to the stigma it feels like today?

> I think that more people need to recognize and embrace singleness as a unique time of life with many advantages. Jesus never got married, so it must be an okay state to be in.
>
> —Suzanne, 28, single

Paul's Wisdom

Sometimes, I feel sorry for Paul. He's the "single guy" of the Bible and will own that label for all time. Even though Paul is the one we usually connect with singleness, the Bible doesn't tell us the marital status of everyone it mentions. I find it interesting that the Bible mainly highlights the stories of individuals, not just couples.

We definitely shouldn't overlook Paul's wisdom and guidance as a single man. As Brant Hansen mentioned, Paul being single was countercultural during his time as well.

I like the wording Paul used at the beginning of the book of Romans to describe himself: "Paul, a servant of Christ Jesus, called to be an apostle and set apart for the gospel of God" (Romans 1:1).

Instead of singles or outsiders, what if we thought of ourselves as set apart for God and servants of Jesus? I know what you're thinking because I'm thinking the same thing. "Wait, I don't want to be single forever like Paul!" I don't want to call myself "set apart" in fear that God will set me apart on this lonely path forever. It doesn't work like that, though. God knows you and every desire in your heart.

I'm challenging you, as a single woman, to see yourself as set apart for this time. Embrace this calling and instead of feeling like a second-class citizen, believe that you're chosen by God to be set apart at this time for a very important reason.

In 1 Corinthians, Paul speaks directly to unmarried people, saying, "Now to the unmarried and the widows I say: It is good for them to stay unmarried, as I do. But if they cannot control themselves, they should marry, for it is better to marry than to burn with passion" (7:8-9).

Why would Paul say it's good to remain single? Explaining himself in the next few paragraphs, he states that "those who marry will face many troubles in this life, and I want to spare you this" (v. 28*b*). In verses 32-35 of the same chapter, Paul explains his views further. Paul tells his readers he wants them to be free from anxieties. He explains that an unmarried woman "is concerned about the Lord's affairs" and "her aim is to be devoted to the Lord in both body and spirit." He continues by saying, "But a married woman is concerned about the affairs of this world—how she can please her husband." He summarizes by recommending "undivided devotion to the Lord."

Friends, these are hard verses for a single person to read. Personally, I spend so much of my time desiring marriage and family, counting the days until I'm chosen by a man who wants to be my husband. How can it be desirable to remain single? I don't desire that at all!

Kendall is a friend of mine who has been engaged for about six months. After many years praying for a husband, she is busy planning her dream wedding. When I talked to her about these verses, she sheepishly admitted she better understands Paul's point of view now. "When I was single, I had to cling to the Lord. My relationship with God was intimate because he was all I had during those hard times." Now that she's engaged, she realizes it is changing her relationship with God. "Sometimes I think my relationship with the Lord is stronger in bad times than during times of abundant blessing."

Does this mean Kendall shouldn't get married? Of course not. She says, "My husband and I desire to serve the Lord together. I know marriage will teach me a lot about love, forgiveness, and sacrifice. It will also be a process of relearning how I relate to God in my new role as a wife."

As singles who desire marriage, it's okay to hope and dream about the future. As long as we're still living in the present and using the time to grow our faith in God. We have a loving God. We need to walk boldly and confidently in his love.

> *Truth: God loves you unconditionally regardless of your marital status, actions, or choices.*

God doesn't see these labels we put on each other. To God, we aren't black or white, male or female, married or single, mother or father. We are beloved children, forgiven and released prisoners, and unconditionally accepted heirs of God.

God Is Love

I wrote the following prayer quite a few years ago as I began to let God show me the fullness of his love for me.

Father, forgive me for believing the lie that you don't love me. Although I've always known that you are love and that you love me, I haven't always understood or comprehended it. I certainly haven't always lived like I believe it. Thank you for bringing me to the realization of your vast, unconditional love. I repent of the lies I have believed. Let me live each day remembering and knowing your vast love for me. Bring me to a greater understanding of it each day. God, you *are* love. Amen.

I know you want God to finish writing your love story. Just like me, you're probably tired of waiting. When singleness feels too heavy to bear for another day, remember that God has already written a love story for you—the one between you and him. He loves you so much he sent his only Son to suffer and die so that you can be reconciled to him. If you were the only sinner who needed redemption, God still would send Jesus to die for you. That is an amazing love.

God's love is the only love that is everlasting. It's the love that will fulfill the deepest desire of our hearts. Because that's the way he created us.

> How dare the enemy whisper the words "you're not loved" to any of God's precious children? God so loved the world that he gave his only Son for us. God's love is unconditional and permanent. His love for us will never cease. That's amazing to think about! Even if no one on this earth ever loved you, you are still loved by the creator of everything. That's huge!
>
> —Liz, 31, single

For a while, I became very touchy and bitter about my singleness. During that time, my friends and fellow church members really couldn't do anything right in my mind. I was super sensitive to any remarks or questions about being single. On my best days, I believed my single journey was one that God ordained for good. On bad days, I was pretty sure he was punishing me for something.

Even though I felt insecure and outcast at church, God taught me something. Since I'm hoping to love a spouse someday and will need to show my husband grace, there is no better place to start practicing love and grace than at church. If people and their comments at church are stepping on my toes, imagine living with someone every single day. Talk about getting your toes squashed. I learned that I needed to step back and start learning to show grace.

God gently nudged me toward love. He prompted me to give people at church the benefit of the doubt and show them grace. Even when they say something that hurts my feelings, it's not intentional. I need to practice love.

I didn't change overnight. I was still overly sensitive about being single during those days. But I started to realize if God could love me through all the times I've hurt his feelings, refused to obey, and turned my back on him, surely I could show a little love and grace to others.

Once we're confident and secure in God's love for us, we can boldly love others. Regardless of marital status, we're called to love others every day. Just like our wise friend Paul says in another of his letters, "If I have a faith that can move mountains, but do not have love, I am nothing" (1 Corinthians 13:2).

• • •

If I speak in the tongues of men or of angels, but do not have love, I am only a resounding gong or a clanging cymbal. If I have the gift of prophecy and can fathom all mysteries and all knowledge, and if I have a faith that can move mountains, but do not have love, I am nothing. If I give all I possess to the poor and give over my body to hardship that I may boast, but do not have love, I gain nothing. (1 Corinthians 13:1-3)

The church values married people more than me.

Women who believe this lie often say:

- I can't get truly involved at my church until I'm married.
- Since I don't have a family, I'm not valuable at church.
- Church members only see me as the single girl who is available to babysit.
- Since the church values marriage and family, God must see me as second class.
- I can't be fully devoted to God until I'm married.

God loves you unconditionally regardless of your marital status, actions, or choices.

God says:

- **You are my beloved children and heirs.**
  Now if we are children, then we are heirs—heirs of God and co-heirs with Christ, if indeed we share in his sufferings in order that we may also share in his glory. (Romans 8:17)
- **I set the lonely in families.**
  God sets the lonely in families, he leads out the prisoners with singing; but the rebellious live in a sun-scorched land. (Psalm 68:6)
- **I love the church.**
  As the Scriptures say, "A man leaves his father and mother and is joined to his wife, and the two are united into one." This is a great mystery, but it is an illustration of the way Christ and the church are one. (Ephesians 5:31-32, NLT)

111

- **I have called you by name and you are mine.**
  But now, O Jacob, listen to the LORD who created you. O Israel, the one who formed you says, "Do not be afraid, for I have ransomed you. I have called you by name; you are mine." (Isaiah 43:1, NLT)

- **I understand your struggles.**
  For we do not have a high priest who is unable to empathize with our weaknesses, but we have one who has been tempted in every way, just as we are—yet he did not sin. (Hebrews 4:15)

Lies I Believe:

Truth I Want to Remember:

9

Lie #9: It's too late for me, so I should settle.

Glancing across the room at the crowded party, I saw my boyfriend laughing and chatting with his friends. I longed to smile and proudly say, "That's my guy." Instead, my stomach muscles clenched in a familiar way. On paper, he's the guy I should marry. He's a great Christian guy who loves God and treats me with respect. He's handsome, successful, and involved in his church. He has a great group of friends and loves to serve others. We were both in our early thirties and ready to settle down. So, what was causing my stomach pains and uneasiness?

When I think back about all of the times I tried to settle, it astounds me. I tried to force so many relationships to work because I believed time was running out. There was nothing wrong with my handsome boyfriend who loved Jesus. I could have stayed in the relationship and possibly even chosen to marry him, but I knew I was forcing it to fit. It would have been a difficult road for me to choose.

The guy who seems perfect on paper may not be the right spouse for you. Of course, we need to know our nonnegotiable characteristics. Your future spouse needs to love God and actively follow him. He needs to treat you with respect. He needs to pursue you. If you find yourself compromising your values to be with him, he's not the guy for you.

Recently, I've seen numerous blog posts about the ten traits you should look for in a husband or the twenty-five characteristics your life partner should possess. Over the years, I've purchased stacks of books about finding the right mate. Choosing a spouse is one of the most important decisions we will make during our lives. We can research the issue and make checklists. But finding the love of your life isn't something that can be accomplished by reading the right articles and setting your mind to the task. If so, I would have been married long ago!

I've learned something about God, though. Instead of making lists and trying to make something work on my own, he wants me to actively pursue him and remain close to him. If I'm walking closely with God, he won't let me make the choice to settle. He has stopped me many times when I tried to stay in relationships for the sake of my own timetable.

> You should be particular. You are a princess and the daughter of the *King!* You are worth walking across the room for.
>
> —*Catherine, 45, married*

Sarah is a thirty-six-year-old single woman who is smart, beautiful, and faithful. Like many of us, she feels tempted to settle. Sarah says, "I want you to know how tempting it is to lower my standards. I get asked out by non-Christian men all the time. I know I'm sending out the right vibe (that I'm open and available and interested), but I want someone whose faith matters to him. Sometimes I feel like I'm choosing between God and my husband."[1]

I agree with Sarah. It's very tempting to start lowering our standards as time passes, especially as our friends find seemingly perfect spouses and we're stuck home alone on Saturday night. On those nights, I try to remember the common advice I've heard over and over during my single journey. "The loneliest place is being stuck in a bad marriage." I realize some women may be criticized for being too selective about dating, but my story is one about not being selective enough.

Refusing to Settle

About ten years ago, I was in a dating relationship with a guy who didn't respect himself and wasn't pursuing God. He went to church because he knew it was important to me, not because it meant something to him. At that particular time in my life, I believed it was enough for me. I was settling for less but didn't want to face the truth. One weekend, I traveled to my hometown because my grandfather was being honored at our home church.

At the ceremony naming him an honorary deacon, I heard many things I already knew about my grandfather, Nandy. He served for decades as a church deacon and Sunday school teacher. But I also learned something new. For years, Nandy led a weekly Bible study at the county jail for the inmates there. He never talked or bragged about how he gave up his time to serve those men.

In the middle of that ceremony, God finally broke through my stubbornness and disobedience. As I looked at my grandfather (who looked like he would rather be sitting in his recliner at home than on that stage being honored), I made a promise to God and myself. I will wait for a man like my grandfather. Nandy lived out love and faith every day as he humbly and quietly served his God and our family. I want to marry someone whose actions are stronger than his words.

Back home, I ended the relationship with my boyfriend who wasn't following the Lord. He wasn't a bad guy. I knew he loved me very much, but I also knew I wanted to marry someone who had a close walk with the Lord.

I wish I could tell you I kept high standards and only made wise relationship choices after that memorable moment. I didn't. In fact, I made some fairly disastrous choices along the way. But when I made bad choices and things fell apart, I always went back to God and relinquished my hopes and dreams at his feet again. My bad choices complicated my journey. I spent years dating the wrong kinds of guys and not loving myself enough to make wise dating decisions. It took me a long time to understand how many of my choices were based on lies I believed about myself, some dating back to early childhood.

My friend Samantha and I discuss this topic frequently. I think being single in our mid-thirties leads us to much self-reflection and analysis. Why are we still single? Samantha and I have each sought advice from Christian counselors, which has been helpful and insightful for both of us.

> God can use us in our singleness, sometimes more than when we are in a relationship. It's just a matter of perspective and whether or not we choose to be open to this fact.
>
> —Jordan, 31, single

Samantha gave me permission to share part of her story with you. "My parents have a very codependent relationship. I grew up in a home with a controlling and verbally abusive father, which gave me a distorted picture of what marriage should look like. Over the years, I've realized that it feels suffocating for someone to need me, and it scares me to need somebody else."

Samantha also admits that her dad's relationship with her mom has caused a lot of insecurity in her life. "Daughters from these types of marriages often doubt their self-value because they have seen their mothers devalued all their lives."

I asked Samantha how these insecurities from her childhood affect her current dating choices. She concluded, "It's hard for me to imagine that someone I love could love me back. I fear having to settle for someone I don't love in order to find someone capable of loving me."

Brenda also shared with me how her family relationships have affected her dating and marriage choices. "Because I had such a rocky relationship with my father, I had a terrible time keeping my standards high." Brenda admitted, "I sought out validation from men. Instead of knowing that God loved me and thought of me as his precious child, I needed a man to do that for me."

After talking to women all over the country, I've heard this theme a lot. Our relationships with our earthly fathers affect many of our choices with men. I'm not saying you should call your father and blame him if you've been single longer than expected or if you have trouble relating to men in dating relationships. But if you think past events or relationships may be affecting your current choices, there are many helpful resources that address this particular issue.

Samantha, Brenda, and I each learned that settling is often a subconscious choice, not something we intentionally set out to do. I can't tell you how many people have warned me over the years not to settle when making choices about dating and marriage. Yet I've learned it takes more than simple instruction not to settle, especially when there are emotional and environmental factors at play, some dating back more than thirty years.

If you believe you need assistance from a Christian mentor or counselor to help you sort through any of these issues, please pray about it and ask friends and pastors for recommendations of local resources. I grew up believing that counselors were for people who were unable to handle their own emotions. That belief caused me to stuff my emotional baggage and prevented me from seeking the counsel I needed for many years. Thankfully, I had friends who were open about their experiences with Christian counselors and pushed me in a direction that changed my life.

If you ask God to take you on a journey of healing, he will do it. You may not know all of the emotional factors that are affecting your relationships, but God does. He desperately wants to show us his love and heal our broken places. As we read in Psalm 147:3: "He heals the brokenhearted and binds up their wounds."

Even when we believe we've wasted all of our chances and it's too late, God always welcomes us to come back to him.

Truth: You can trust God with your life.

*Y*ou're completely safe in his arms. You can trust him, remain close to him, and abide in him. Relying on God is the key to achieving peace in our dating lives and preventing us from settling.

God Is Peace

We all want more peace in our lives. Most of my single girl-friends would love to have less anxiety about dating and fret less about who their future spouse may be and when marriage might happen. The guy you ultimately marry should be the one who gives you a sense of peace and security, the one who loves you as Jesus Christ loves his church.

In the book of John, Jesus gives us words of peace: "Peace I leave with you; my peace I give you. I do not give to you as the world gives. Do not let your hearts be troubled and do not be afraid" (John 14:27).

Relying on this peace that Jesus promises means letting go of my right to do everything I want. When I am troubled, frustrated, or afraid, it's usually because I am asserting my rights. "God, I have a *right* to get married before I'm forty and have children. I have a *right* to be happy in this area of my life." But do I really?

I am a sinner saved by the blood of Jesus Christ. I deserve to be punished for my sins. Instead, God sent Jesus to pay the price. I am given a free gift of grace and mercy, not rights to happiness or marriage. I desire those good things, and God loves to give his children gifts, but I must give up my sense of entitlement. In exchange, he gives me a beautiful sense of peace.

Questions from Jesus

Accepting the peace Jesus offers us is a daily choice. It means resting in him and knowing that he will take care of us and our needs. It requires faith.

There is a story in the ninth chapter of Matthew that I've heard since childhood but recently understood in a new way. Two blind men approached Jesus and boldly entered the house where he was staying. They begged him for healing and mercy. Jesus responded with a question. "Do you believe that I am able to do this?" (Matthew 9:28b).

On the surface, it seems like a simple question. Do you believe? The men say yes and Jesus heals them. But the question is not simple at all. On a daily basis, Jesus is asking each of us whether we believe him.

Do you believe that . . .

I can be trusted with your heart?
I will fulfill my promises to you?
I will heal your brokenness?
I will provide what you need?
I will never let you go?

Of course, I want to answer Jesus with a wholehearted reply. "Yes, Lord. I believe!" Even though I say it with my mouth, some days I keep living like I don't believe him—like I'm still blind. This is a prayer I wrote when I was struggling to believe, when I feared I may have to settle to fulfill my dreams of being married:

Lord, help my unbelief. I choose to believe; help me overcome my unbelief (Mark 9:24).

Help me release control and get out of the way of your plans.

Help me to let go of the past and the people in my past.

Help me to be able to turn toward the unknown and lean into you.

Help me to surrender my plans and priorities to you.

Calm my fears; teach me to rest in you.

Lord, teach me to believe.

• • •

Trusting the Lord with your life requires courage. It means stepping out of our comfort zones in faith and giving up our rights. Don't believe the lie that you must lower your standards to be married. Instead of settling, let's choose to believe in God's peace. Instead of acting out of fear, let's walk closely with God and live as children of his light.

• • •

For you were once darkness, but now you are light in the Lord.
Live as children of light (for the fruit of the light consists in
all goodness, righteousness and truth) and find out what
pleases the Lord. (Ephesians 5:8-10)

It's too late for me, so I should settle.

Women who believe this lie often say:

- It's okay for me to date this guy who doesn't love God; I will be a good influence on him.
- This relationship has to work; I can't start over again at my age.
- My friends and family say I'm too picky, so I need to lower my standards.
- In my heart, something is missing with this guy, but he loves me. I can't have it all.

You can trust God with your life.

God says:

- **Choose a husband who will love you as Christ loved the church.**
  Husbands, love your wives, just as Christ loved the church and gave himself up for her. (Ephesians 5:25)

- **Wait patiently in hope for what you do not have.**
  For in this hope we were saved. But hope that is seen is no hope at all. Who hopes for what they already have? But if we hope for what we do not yet have, we wait for it patiently. (Romans 8:24-25)

- **Ask for my advice and know that my purpose will prevail.**
  Listen to advice and accept discipline, and at the end you will be counted among the wise. Many are the plans in a person's heart, but it is the LORD's purpose that prevails. (Proverbs 19:20-21)

- **Renew your mind and search for my pleasing and perfect will.**
  Do not conform to the pattern of this world, but be transformed by the renewing of your mind. Then you will be able to test and approve what God's will is—his good, pleasing and perfect will. (Romans 12:2)

Lies I Believe:

....

....

....

....

....

....

....

....

....

Truth I Want to Remember:

....

....

....

....

....

....

....

....

....

10

Lie #10: My life is on hold until I find a spouse.

*ℐ*ournal entry from Tuesday, September 11, 2007:

Cinque Terre, Italy . . .

I woke up feeling refreshed and so glad to be here in Italy. This really is paradise, the most beautiful place I have ever seen. Even though I'm here by myself, I'm not lonely at all. I truly needed this quiet time for my soul. And I have seven more nights here at this hotel, so I don't have to rush and do everything I want to do now. I decided to stay in bed awhile just relaxing. After a typical Italian breakfast (croissants, granola, yogurt, latte), I'm now sitting in the solarium outside the hotel. It's a patio area with sun chairs and umbrellas right on the edge of this cliff overlooking the village and the sea. Not to exaggerate, but this may be the most peaceful place on earth. Sitting here with this view, listening to the waves, hearing church bells toll every so often . . . what an amazing place to be still, reflect, and pray.

In 2007, I traveled to Italy by myself on a relaxing vacation. Ever since I read *Eat, Pray, Love* by Elizabeth Gilbert, I wanted to take a solo trip to Italy. I'm definitely not an extrovert, so I knew spending ten days alone wouldn't be a problem. Plus, I was deeply tired—physically, emotionally, and spiritually. I needed rest and solitude.

I was single, about to turn thirty-two, and tired of putting my life on hold while waiting on a husband. I didn't want to save any more trips for after I was married. For those of us who desire to be married, it's tempting to hit the pause button on life and put our plans on hold.

When I bought my first home, a condominium in Nashville, I was twenty-six years old. I remember confidently telling my real estate agent that I wouldn't live in the condo too long because I would be getting married within the next five years. She asked, "Oh, are you dating someone?" Sheepishly, I admitted I wasn't. But I just *knew* that I would be married before the age of thirty. (I lived in that condo for eleven-and-a-half years, by the way.)

As women, most of us think about the future and how our choices will affect our future spouse. Making thoughtful decisions is a good thing. I want my future husband making wise choices now that won't negatively impact me in the future. And I should do the same. But sometimes we get carried away with the future and forget to live in the present. I asked some of my single friends for examples of how they've put their lives on hold waiting for marriage.

Kristi admits, "For a while, I didn't want to buy furniture because I just assumed that I would get married soon and we would buy new things together. That's a very basic example, but it's true. I finally gave up and just bought the furniture."

Suzanne hesitated to move overseas or to a new city without the security of a spouse. "I want to share the experience of living in a new place with a spouse, and I would like a male partner to help me reach out to other couples in the new city. A husband would also make a great safety companion when overseas."

For years, I purchased cheap cookware, plates, and glasses because I was certain that I would have a bridal registry someday. It sounds silly, but all of my friends got their "good stuff" from their wedding registries. I was relieved to discover I'm not the only one who subscribed to this line of thinking. Brooke responded to my survey and said, "Sometimes I don't want to buy too many household or kitchen items, because if I own everything, what will I put on my bridal registry?"

When I turned thirty, I was fed up with cheap kitchen accessories, especially since I spend a lot of time cooking. I started asking my friends and family to give me nice plates, serving items, and cookware for birthdays and Christmas gifts. I realize some of these examples may sound minor or petty, but it's easy to let this thought pattern carry over to more important areas as well.

Some of the women I interviewed mentioned their careers, which made me think about my choices in that area. Because I wasn't married, I used my career to establish my value and fill the void I felt. I climbed the corporate ladder because it was a place for me to spend my time and hide my insecurities about being single. I was intrigued to hear some different outlooks from other women on this topic:

> I don't want to advance too far in my career sometimes because if I were to meet a man, would he be able to handle that?
>
> —*Brooke, single, 25*

• • •

> There have been times when I felt like I needed to choose between a career and waiting for a husband so I could be a wife and mom instead.
>
> —*Liz, 31, single*

• • •

It's tempting for us to believe the lie that we need to put our lives on hold until we're married. Whether it's a romantic place we want to visit or a mortgage, we didn't picture doing it alone. It's hard to let go of those dreams and admit that we may not have a husband with whom to share these life events.

I also interviewed some single men about the temptation women face to put their lives on hold while waiting for marriage. Craig admitted this issue is not exclusive to women. "Do not put your life on hold. I did this, and it only resulted in wasted years." Craig is forty-three and told me that he started living life to its fullest when he placed his trust in God. As advice to single women, Craig wisely stated, "If you're putting your life on hold for a spouse, you are putting unfair pressure on that individual, and he will never be able to live up to your expectations."

Mack is a single, twenty-five-year-old guy who has a strong opinion on this topic. He said, "A real man doesn't want to marry a woman who has put her life on hold. He wants to be married to a complete woman." Mack wants a woman who will put an appropriate focus on him, but he also wants her to have her own goals and passions. "I want to marry a real person who has experiences I've never had and brings something to the table, something that makes me more complete and a better man." Mack advises, "Don't put your life on hold. Take this time to experience life so you can bring that into your marriage and have more to offer as a wife."

A Rich and Satisfying Life

Marriage is not a prerequisite for enjoying life or serving God. Take that trip to Europe. Buy a house. Use the nice china for dinner. Don't wait until you are married to enjoy life. When you meet your spouse, you'll be able to tell him about the experiences that made you the well-rounded and interesting person you have become.

> *Truth: God desires for you to live an abundant life every day through faith in Jesus Christ.*

In the book of John, Jesus says, "My purpose is to give them a rich and satisfying life" (John 10:10*b*, NLT). Not a rich and satisfying life *once they get married*. In this chapter, Jesus calls himself the gate and says that anyone who enters through him will be saved. He is the only prerequisite to an abundant life. Since he's offering it, I think we should take him up on it.

A rich and satisfying life doesn't mean every day is going to be happy and joyful. There have been some really dark days during my single journey. I have experienced days when I wasn't sure God would answer my prayers and weeks when hope was hanging by a thread. There have been long periods of time when I couldn't hear God at all, when I wanted to give up and settle for less than what my heart longed for.

There have also been times when I felt intimately close to God, like he was sitting next to me at the breakfast table. Other times, I knew he was there, but it felt like a blanket was covering me. I couldn't feel God's presence, even though I clung to his promises to never leave me. It felt very dark and I struggled to pray.

I remembered a story from the Old Testament when Moses and Joshua were fighting the Amalekites. In Exodus 17, we pick up the story: "Moses, Aaron and Hur went to the top of the hill. As long as Moses held up his hands, the Israelites were winning, but whenever he lowered his hands, the Amalekites were winning" (vv. 10*b*-11).

Everything was going well until Moses got tired. But Moses wasn't on the hill alone: "When Moses' hands grew tired, they took a stone and put it under him and he sat on it. Aaron and Hur held his hands up—one on one side, one on the other—so that his hands remained steady till sunset. So Joshua overcame the Amalekite army with the sword" (vv. 12-13).

We get tired of standing with our arms raised, too, don't we? We're tired of being single, tired of doing it all ourselves, and simply exhausted from the dark times when we can't feel God's presence. We don't have to be on the hill alone. Don't be afraid to find your Aaron and Hur. Reach out to your friends and ask them to hold you up.

During that dark time when I couldn't pray, I emailed some of my close friends. I told them I was struggling, that I was angry with God, and that I couldn't even pray. I specifically noted the story in Exodus 17 and asked them to stand beside me and pray on my behalf. I told them I couldn't do it by myself anymore.

Their prayers carried me until I was able to talk to God again. During some of those darkest times, I was often drawn to these verses in Psalm 30: "Sing to the LORD, all you godly ones! Praise his holy name. For his anger lasts only a moment, but his favor lasts a lifetime! *Weeping may last through the night, but joy comes with the morning*" (vv. 4-5, NLT, emphasis mine).

Honestly, that last promise made me angry. I didn't understand it. After nights of sadness or weeping, I woke up expecting joy—sometimes demanding my joy—but it wasn't there. *God, why do you keep giving me this promise of joy in the morning when I can't find my way out of the darkness?*

Over time, I learned that God's definition of "night" is different from ours. Our night of weeping may go on for months or even years. His timing is not our timing, and his ways are not our ways. On those dark days when life doesn't seem very abundant, God is with us in the darkness and through the weeping. "Though I sit in darkness, the LORD will be my light" (Micah 7:8*b*).

And God *will* bring joy in the morning. It's a promise and you can cling to it. We serve the God who makes all things possible, the one who specializes in resurrections of hope. You can trust your heart to God. He is the one who chases after you with his love and grace. He won't let go of you.

God as Giver

God wants to give us full lives. The abundant, rich life he gives comes from being in relationship with him. It's a result of trusting him in both the dark times and the joyful ones. It definitely doesn't come by him giving us everything we ask at the moment we ask for it. God wants us to love him and seek a relationship with him because of who he is, not because of what he can give us.

In his book *Crazy Love*, Francis Chan said, "The greatest knowledge we can ever have is knowing God treasures us."[1] Chan talks about how Jesus wants us and chooses us. The satisfaction of walking with God comes when we realize what he desires from us. So, what does God want? He wants a relationship with us.

Throughout Scripture, God is identified as a giver. Psalm 84:11 (NLT) reads, "For the LORD God is our sun and our shield. He gives us grace and glory." In another of my favorite verses, the Bible reads, "Every good and perfect gift is from above, coming down from the Father of the heavenly lights, who does not change like shifting shadows" (James 1:17).

> The best advice that changed my life was in the form of a quote by Leonard Cohen. "If you don't become the ocean, you'll be seasick every day." I had to learn to stop fighting my singleness; it was making me seasick!
>
> —Kristi, 33, single

God's ultimate gift came when he sacrificed his Son so that we may be forgiven for our sins and have an eternal relationship with him. In relationships, we desire to give the best of ourselves to each other. Examining the extent of the sacrifice God made for us, it only makes sense that he desires to continue giving us good things.

Even though God is present during each step of my journey and cares about the unmet desires of my heart, I sometimes struggle to believe his promises. I know he holds me in his hand, but seemingly unanswered prayers take a toll on my view of God's goodness.

One area where I particularly struggle is feeling as if I'm not doing enough to fulfill my desire of getting married. Some time ago, I joined an online dating service because I felt I should do something active about my desire for marriage. I cancelled my subscription after six months because it wasn't right for me. I went on lots of dates with guys I met online, but the concept of corresponding in detail with someone before meeting him face-to-face didn't work out well for me. I do have many friends who met online and have great marriages, so I'm not saying it won't work for you!

Also, I feel guilty when I don't go to every event I'm invited to attend. What if that's the party where I would have met my husband, but I chose to stay home and read a book? Sometimes, I torture myself with "what ifs." I know God wants to give me good things. Am I doing enough to put myself in the right situations at the right times? It's exhausting to believe I'm solely in control.

We tend to think God is limited, don't we? My view of God's power is limited when I fear I've missed my future spouse because I don't attend every singles event at church. There have been times when I became certain my poor choices led me down a path of remaining single for the rest of my life. I carried so much regret and believed I brought this prolonged singleness on myself because I wasn't following God closely enough or working hard enough on my issues.

A bold friend confronted me about this lie. Looking into my eyes, she asked, "Do you think you're more powerful than God?" Reacting strongly, I told her I most certainly did not believe that. She helped me realize I was carrying the burden myself instead of resting in God. She led me to pray and release the tight grip I held on my vision for the "perfect life." She inspired me to turn my regrets over to God and ask for his guidance in my dating life.

Slowly, I'm learning to stop focusing on what I don't have and enjoy the fun and freedom my single life has to offer. When I trust God for the present moment, I'm able to let go of my anxieties about the future.

> Most people will get married at some point in their lives, so we need to start liking our single lives instead of always wishing we were married.
>
> —Suzanne, 28, single

If we were sitting across from each other drinking a cup of coffee, I would tell you to believe in the goodness of God. In spite of your feelings, when it's difficult to see through the fog, when your faith is being tested, when prayers seemingly go unanswered, and when your dreams don't come true, just believe. God is still there, and he loves you more than you can imagine. God cares about the details of your life. He cares about whom you choose to marry. Trust him while you wait for the desires of your heart.

Waiting is difficult, but it always has a purpose. Years of waiting on a spouse is teaching me to rely on God. My faith is stronger because my desires haven't been immediately fulfilled. I am learning to depend on God to give me peace. I'm learning to trust him to bring me good things, even if those things look a bit different than I expected.

This time in the waiting room of singleness is building my faith in God and preparing me for something. Marriage? I truly hope so. But even if that desire isn't met in this life, I know there will be no unfulfilled desires in heaven. I choose to put my dreams in the capable hands of God and let him fulfill my needs.

I challenge you to do the same. Believe in the goodness of God. Seek a relationship with God because you want *him*, not what he can give you. Then, receive God's overflowing blessings of love, grace, and truth, as he provides the good things he knows you need.

As his cherished children, let's live full and abundant lives each day, focusing on God's truth and refusing to believe lies about ourselves and about God.

• • •

The LORD your God is with you, the Mighty Warrior who saves. He will take great delight in you; in his love he will no longer rebuke you, but will rejoice over you with singing. (Zephaniah 3:17)

My life is on hold until I find a spouse.

Women who believe this lie often say:

- I want to take a trip to _____, but it's a romantic place. I would rather save that trip until I'm married.
- I don't want to buy a house on my own without a spouse.
- My future husband may not want me to have this type of career.
- I will wait until I'm married to _____ (invest in nice furniture, buy nice dishes, etc.).
- My life will start when I find someone to marry.

God desires for you to live an abundant life every day through faith in Jesus Christ.

God says:

- **Put your hope in me.**
  Command those who are rich in this present world not to be arrogant nor to put their hope in wealth, which is so uncertain, but to put their hope in God, who richly provides us with everything for our enjoyment. (1 Timothy 6:17)
- **Work with enthusiasm at whatever you do.**
  Work willingly at whatever you do, as though you were working for the Lord rather than for people. (Colossians 3:23, NLT)
- **Give your requests to me; don't be anxious.**
  Do not be anxious about anything, but in every situation, by prayer and petition, with thanksgiving, present your requests to God. And the peace of God, which transcends all understanding, will guard your hearts and your minds in Christ Jesus. (Philippians 4:6-7)

Lies I Believe:

....

....

....

....

....

....

....

....

Truth I Want to Remember:

....

....

....

....

....

....

....

....

Conclusion

In writing this book, I chose the top ten lies I personally believed throughout my years of singleness. You may have believed the same lies or possibly different ones. Regardless, the battle of replacing lies with truth is one that's common to all Christians, regardless of marital status.

Throughout the book, each chapter highlighted specific character traits of God. In addition to all of these traits, God is our ultimate Truth. When we start believing lies, we must turn to him and his Word for truth.

The truth about who God is . . .

God is our Companion, Provider, and Hope (chapter 1).

God is Faithful and Trustworthy (chapter 2).

God is our Shepherd (chapter 3).

God is our Redeemer and Healer (chapter 4).

God is Creator (chapter 5).

God (through Jesus) is our Savior (chapter 6).

God is Abba Father (chapter 7).

God is Love (chapter 8).

God is Peace (chapter 9).

God is a Giver (chapter 10).

Who is God? He is everything on this list and so much more. He is our true light. God only asks that we believe in his name and receive his grace through Jesus. Then, we inherit the extraordinary right to become his children and to have a relationship with our Father who is full of grace and truth:

The true light that gives light to everyone was coming into the world. He was in the world, and though the world was made through him, the world did not recognize him. He came to that which was his own, but his own did not receive him. *Yet to all who did receive him, to those who believed in his name, he gave the right to become children of God—children born not of natural descent, nor of human decision or a husband's will, but born of God.* The Word became flesh and made his dwelling among us. We have seen his glory, the glory of the one and only Son, who came from the Father, full of grace and truth (John 1:9-14, emphasis mine).

This is the ultimate love story, the one woven through every chapter of the Bible. There is truly no end to God's affection for you.

When you're struggling with believing lies, when you don't feel cherished or valuable, when you feel forgotten or lost, or when you're not sure what to believe, I pray you will seek God and ask him, "Who are you?" He will reveal himself. He is the author of your story, and he craves a relationship with you.

BONUS SECTIONS

Single Men Respond

What single woman hasn't wondered what single guys are thinking? As I wrote this book, I became curious whether single men also struggled with believing lies. If so, I wondered if they battled the same lies women face. Since I was in a unique position to ask these questions, I created a survey for single men between the ages of twenty-five and fifty-five who identified themselves as followers of Christ.

In full disclosure, I also allowed some recently married men to complete the survey. I know these particular guys and asked them to answer the questions. These specific men were single a long time, and I value their input based on their single years. I think it adds depth to their responses because they are looking back upon their single journey as married men.

The results shared below are based on twenty completed surveys. Below, I have given you the exact question I asked in the survey and then a summary of responses.

What Lies Do Single Men Believe?

Question posed: As a single man, which of the following statements have you believed at one time or another? (Check as many as apply.) Note: These are statements that I, as a single woman, believed to be true at one time or another that I now recognize to be lies.

Answers: With 65 percent of the men surveyed choosing it as one of their answers, the most common statement believed by single men was: "I'm not attractive." In second place, 55 percent of respondents chose: "There is something wrong with me." At 50 percent, the third-most-selected statement was "Sex outside of marriage is okay."

The remainder of the statements ranked as follows. The percentage of respondents who chose each statement is shown.

- Because no one has chosen me, I'm not valuable. (40 percent)
- Getting married will solve all my problems. (35 percent)
- My church values married people more than me. (35 percent)
- My life is on hold until I find a spouse. (30 percent)
- It's too late for me, so I should settle. (30 percent)
- God has forgotten about me. (25 percent)
- My past can't be forgiven. (20 percent)
- I haven't believed any of these lies/statements. (15 percent)

Question posed: The list of statements above was specifically written with single women in mind. What is missing from this list? As a single man, what other lies have you believed about yourself?

Sample of answers:

I don't make enough money. I'm not good enough for the "type" of woman I want/need.

—Josh, 30, single

• • •

I have always believed that the separation between myself and the "ideal guy" is a far greater distance than I cross. What I believe women want in a man (tall, dark, handsome) is simply an idealistic image from culture, not reality.

—Gavin, 32, single

• • •

I'm not successful enough. I don't have a lot of fun things to offer. I can't seem to "lead" the women I date (as they describe often in the church).

—Jake, 36, single

• • •

I'm old-fashioned and out-of-touch. I am too picky.

—Lawrence, 45, single

• • •

I will be too old to be a parent if I don't hurry up. I must be too picky. I need to move ahead even if I do not have God's peace about a relationship.

—*Craig, 43, single*

• • •

Maybe I wasn't meant for marriage.

—*Mack, 25, single*

• • •

I have to change my physical appearance to find a girlfriend or wife (i.e., work out and be muscular). I need to settle for less, not a good pretty Christian girl. The vehicle I drive will help me get a girl.

—*Thomas, 32, married*

• • •

I am somehow less of a Christian and not qualified to serve or lead others (because I'm not married).

—*Phil, 43, single*

• • •

Author Commentary

I was surprised to learn that single men struggle with many of the same issues women do, especially with self-image. With 65 percent of respondents choosing "I am not attractive" as a statement they have believed, this appears to be an insecurity that we all battle. As a single woman, I tend to believe guys are confident most of the time and have less insecurity than I do. It's comforting for me to know that guys struggle with many of the same questions and fears I face on a daily basis.

What Do Single Men Think About Premarital Sex?

Question posed: Regarding premarital sex, do you believe it's important to wait until marriage to have sex? Why or why not?

Sample of answers:

Yes, because it's an important symbol of a sacred bond.

—*Nate, 30, single*

• • •

Yes, I think people should wait. God intended sex to be the closest bond a man and woman can ever have together. As a result, the emotional damage it can cause by having multiple partners before marriage is huge for the level of ultimate intimacy with one person. It also wreaks havoc and complicates the dating process (i.e., unplanned pregnancy, negative emotions) and can hinder the blessings God could have on the spiritual relationship of the couple. Speaking from experience in this area, I do believe God can heal and restore those who have had sex outside marriage.

—*Jake, 36, single*

• • •

It is important to wait. I view marriage as an important commitment between two people in Christ. Sex is a powerful act between people that shouldn't be regarded lightly.

—*Marcus, 26, single*

• • •

Completely important to wait. Sex is truly the superglue for souls in marriage. I have never in all my years as a marriage and family therapist encountered a couple who said, "All my premarital sex has really been a boon for my marriage." In fact, I have frequently seen the opposite. In this day and age where unrestricted sexual expression is promoted as a moral good, taking a stand to remain celibate until marriage is a way to loudly proclaim by example what we believe to be true.

—*Caleb, 37, married*

• • •

Theologically, I know it is wrong. My own life has shown me it only causes death. So with that in mind, I would say yes. But to be honest, a lie I confront a lot is that sex outside of marriage is okay.

—*Roberto, 27, single*

• • •

Premarital sexual activity is nothing more than shortsighted pleasure in the moment. It's easy to fall into it when we are not keeping our sights on the long term. The benefits are short-term, but the repercussions can last a lifetime.

—*Thomas, 32, married*

• • •

I do believe it is important to wait, although I do not believe that a relationship is either saved or destroyed by it. Sex requires open communication to be enjoyed, and waiting until those communication skills are learned/developed is critical. Getting married does not construct these skills, but honesty, time, and a shared willingness to learn does.

—*Gavin, 32, single*

• • •

Yes, for several reasons. One, I believe it is something commanded by God. Two, marriage is such an intimate relationship in all aspects (physical, emotional, spiritual, etc.), and marriage is a binding commitment. I only want to share the extreme physical intimacy with that one person with whom I want to share the other intimate aspects of life. And third, a belief that sex is for the marriage bed is part of who I am. I still hold on to the hope of meeting someone special, and it could happen to-morrow or in forty years in a nursing home. But it is still a hope.

—*Lawrence, 45, single*

• • •

God gave us sex as cement between a male and a female, hus-band and wife. Sex is the most intimate act available to humans. While sex is physical, it's only so much so. I'd say maybe 5 to 10 percent. The other 90 percent encompasses emotional, mental, and mostly spiritual intimacy. Premarital sex cannot be true sex.

—*Mack, single, 29*

• • •

Author Commentary

Many of these guys expressed themselves better than I did in chapter 3 regarding this topic. I included these quotes to encourage you that there are single guys out there who believe in the impor-tance of waiting until marriage for sex. And even if they (or you) have made mistakes in the past, I completely agree with Jake: "God can heal and restore those who have had sex outside marriage." I included a variety of the opinions that were expressed, and overall, I was encouraged and challenged by the words of these men. (And no, I didn't ask for their phone numbers in the survey. Sorry, ladies!)

How Does God Factor into a Single Man's Life?

Question posed: In what ways has your Christian faith shaped your journey as a single man? How has God played a role in your single-ness?

Sample of answers:

My Christian values have shaped my single journey as a man by giving me a place to go emotionally when totally defeated by the "single game." Guys get burned too, sometimes in dev-astating ways. I always tried to lean on God when broken and attempted to use that time to increase my faith in him. Even if I did not feel like trusting him, I always tried to simply be thankful.

—*Gavin, 32, single*

• • •

Being single allowed me time to really learn that American masculinity was far adrift from biblical manhood. I realized that so much of what was valued as a man had absolutely no scriptural and spiritual significance. Now as a married man and father, I seek to shape my boys into men who reflect the cross instead of this world.

—*Caleb, 37, married*

• • •

It has brought me closer to God in many ways because I have to do things myself and don't really have someone to rely on as a single person. Because I'm single and live alone, God has brought me peace and contentment in my loneliness and provided great social opportunities to satisfy that as well. God has showed me in my singleness how to be content and filled with the spirit so I'm strong and peaceful. It's not easy, though.

—*Jake, 36, single*

• • •

He keeps the hope alive. He keeps me moving on when it hurts to be single. He keeps giving me a desire when I want to give up on the whole dating thing out of fear of being hurt once again. He is the rock to stand on, even when I don't recognize it at times.

—*Lawrence, 45, single*

• • •

My Christian faith has played a huge role in my journey. In submitting to Christ, I have learned much about life. God has brought me far on this journey, and he teaches me more every day. I have chosen to stay with him and trust him, and he has never let me down. Even during the darkest, loneliest, and emptiest times of my life, I stayed with him, and he brought me to a higher place. The road is sometimes very difficult, but the blessings that follow by staying with God are far greater!

—*Craig, 43, single*

• • •

I can be thankful that this is God's plan for my life. Regardless of my circumstances or emotions, he is still who he says he is. And if I rest in him, I don't have to worry. Not that I operate from that place a lot, but when I do, I have peace.

—*Roberto, 27, single*

• • •

Once I let everything go and put God solely in charge of my life as a single person, I found true happiness.

—*Sam, 42, married*

• • •

My Christian faith is my singleness. I became and stayed single because of it. I felt like God was telling me that I was just throwing my heart around and not only hurting myself but damaging it for my future wife. I wanted to make sure my heart wasn't beholden to anyone but God when I finally meet my wife. . . .

God's love is the most important thing. He is teaching me every day that his love is sufficient and more than enough for me. This is important before I get married so that I don't put love burdens on my wife that she can't fulfill. God is aligning my love expectations so that my marriage can be healthy.

—*Mack, 25, single*

• • •

Looking back, God used every experience and heartache to mold and shape me into the man I needed to be, at the very moment I needed to be. It was so hard to trust him so many times. Looking back, he never left me alone; he was right there.

—*Thomas, 32, married*

• • •

Author Commentary

Again, I hope you're encouraged by these insightful responses from single men. It's interesting to see a common theme of leaning on God and learning to trust him, even though the respondents ranged in age from twenty-five to forty-five years old. Since none of these guys have read the book you're holding, I was astonished to see many of the themes discussed in the book show up here, including resting in God and the peace that believing in God can bring us.

How Often Do Single Men Think about Marriage?

Question posed: Thinking back over the different periods of time in your singleness, please rate how much of the time you thought or believed statements similar to these:

1. I think about marriage often; I'm concerned it might not happen soon enough.
2. I'm content but looking, ready to be married.
3. I'm just enjoying the single life, not too preoccupied about marriage.
4. I'm not sure I ever want to get married.

Answers:

1. I think about marriage often; I'm concerned it might not happen soon enough.

   55 percent answered "some of the time."

   25 percent answered "seldom."

   15 percent answered "most of the time."

   5 percent answered "never."

2. I'm content but looking, ready to be married.

50 percent answered "some of the time."

30 percent answered "most of the time."

10 percent answered "seldom."

10 percent answered "never."

3. I'm just enjoying the single life, not too preoccupied about marriage.

45 percent answered "seldom."

35 percent answered "some of the time."

20 percent answered "most of the time."

0 percent answered "never."

4. I'm not sure I ever want to get married.

60 percent answered "never."

20 percent answered "seldom."

15 percent answered "some of the time."

5 percent answered "most of the time."

Author Commentary

My intent behind this question was to gauge a general feeling about how often single men think about marriage. Are they concerned it won't happen soon enough like I am? Or do most of these guys live contently while waiting for the right person to come along?

This one is difficult to summarize since we could look at it many ways, including factoring in age and looking at individual quotes based on the responses to these four statements. It encouraged me that the majority of guys indicated they were thinking about marriage and/or ready for marriage (statements 1 and 2) some or most of the time. I found it helpful to see this data and consider it along with the other responses in this section.

Advice from Single Men

Question posed: Refer back to the list of lies that single women believe. (Author's note: these are the ten lies included as chapters in this book.) What advice would you give to single, Christian women who struggle with these lies on a daily basis?

Sample of answers:

You are deeply loved by God, and your value comes from him. If you have made mistakes, you can be forgiven and start again. If any man tells you anything different from this, run as fast as you can from him. He will only bring you down and is not the right one for you. If a man is pressuring you to have sex, he also is not the man for you. If he loves you, he will not force sex on you. Instead, if he really loves you, he will respect you. He will want to be with you for the right reasons. Above all, trust God.

—*Craig, 43, single*

• • •

Be faithful to God in all circumstances.

—*Jonathan, 31, married*

• • •

I would tell single women that they are not alone. There are plenty of guys who are feeling the same way and having the same thoughts/fears that they are. . . . [God] has not forgotten about you, and he hears your desires and prayers.

—*Thomas, 32, married*

• • •

"Because no one has chosen me, I am not valuable." From my experience with close friends and past relationships, this is one of the lies I feel is the most prevalent. I've heard so many girls say "she is so lucky" when referring to someone in a relationship with a good guy. If the thinking can be shifted from depending on luck to find a good guy to "I deserve a good guy," this may combat the feelings of weakened self-value. You are worthy and deserving of a guy who will value you, but you have to value yourself first or you may not recognize or trust it when it happens.

—*Gavin, 32, single*

• • •

I've dated many women and have been hurt because many of them didn't know who they were or what they wanted. That's a problem when seeking a relationship. It also opens the door for low self-worth and self-doubt from a woman. Be thankful to God daily for who he has made you to be and how he is shaping you. Many of the other things are out of your control.

—Jake, 36, single

• • •

If you are waiting for someone else's actions through a relationship with you to dictate how complete or loved you feel, you're waiting in vain. Instead, live an interesting, fun, meaningful, purposeful, and godly life and you will attract others who value those qualities.

—Joel, 32, single

• • •

My advice is that it's okay to long for a mate and to hurt. I think it is dangerous to go down an "acceptance" route. Be honest with your desires. Life happens. People get in car wrecks, get laid off . . . and some people are single. God cries with us, and he knows our pain. But we as Christians have the advantage of something to lean on, and even carry us, during times when life does not happen like we wanted. That is the only thing that will keep your feet grounded.

—Lawrence, 45, single

• • •

God has not forgotten about you. . . . A man can reflect God's love to you, but only God can pour true love into you, a love that is sustaining. Because at the end of the day, he created you and what the Creator thinks of you is what truly matters.

—Mack, 25, single

• • •

I love you and am rooting for you. God adores you. You are worthy of love. Give yourself a break. The world you and I live in is like a sea of deception. Deceitful messages wash over us every day, and we must take an active role in reminding ourselves of what is true.

—Alex, 33, single

• • •

The only weapon against a lie is the truth. Remind yourself of the truth.

—Phil, 43, single

Author Commentary

I'm so grateful to these twenty men who were willing to answer these questions openly and share their insight with us. I found so much beauty, truth, and encouragement in the responses given by these men. Unless the respondent specifically requested otherwise, all names have been changed to maintain anonymity.

A Prayer for the Single Woman

Dear Father God,

I lift up my dear reader to you. I pray for her heart to be at peace. I pray you will mend any broken pieces of her heart. We know you are close to the brokenhearted (Psalm 34:18). You are our Healer. You forgive all our sins and heal our diseases (Psalm 103:3). Thank you for pouring out your love and compassion on us (Psalm 103:4).

Lord, I pray in the name of Jesus for any remaining ties to unhealthy relationships—both physical and emotional—to be broken. I pray for peace and closure to surround any hurtful relationships from her past. Meet her in her loneliness and hold her in your arms. She is your beautiful daughter, a co-heir with Christ (Romans 8:17). I pray she will feel your arms holding her tonight and every lonely night.

I pray for hope to be deeply instilled in my friend's heart. As Psalm 33:20 reads, "We wait in hope for the LORD; he is our help and our shield." We wait for you, Lord. We put ourselves and our futures in your hands. We believe you will do a powerful work with and through our lives. We submit our plans to you. Line up our plans with your plans. God, your plans are greater and your ways higher.

I pray for this dear woman to be present in each moment. Allow her to release the regrets of yesterday and focus on the current day. Lord, I pray she will leave the past in your hands and step out into her amazing future with you.

Finally, dear Father, I pray she will not believe lies. As she is attacked by lies regarding her worth, single status, appearance, and any other area, I pray she will seek truth. The truth is clear. She is your daughter, chosen by you. You created her in your image, and you don't make mistakes. Standing alone with nothing to offer, she is enough for you. Each day, may she remember and realize her tremendous value as your child.

In the holy name of Jesus,
Amen

Notes

Chapter 1

1. Oswald Chambers, *My Utmost for His Highest* (Grand Rapids, MI: Discovery House, 2012), May 21.

2. Donald Miller, "Grappling with Control and the Fear of Dying," Donald Miller (blog), March 24, 2011, http://donmilleris.com/2011/03/24/grappling-with-control-and-the-fear-of-dying/.

Chapter 2

1. Leslie Haskin, *God Has Not Forgotten About You: . . . and He Cares More than You Can Imagine* (Minneapolis: Bethany House, 2009), 196.

2. Nancy Wilson, *Why Isn't a Pretty Girl like You Married? and Other Useful Comments* (Moscow, ID: Canon Press, 2010), 11.

Chapter 3

1. Many of these statements were taken from anonymous responses to a survey sent by the author in January 2011 to single and married Christian women, ages twenty-five to fifty. Many of the names have been changed to protect the identities of the respondents.

2. Rebecca St. James with Dale Reeves, *Wait for Me: Rediscovering the Joy of Purity in Romance* (Nashville: Thomas Nelson, 2002), 134.

3. I am thankful to Carter Crenshaw, senior pastor at West End Community Church, in Nashville, Tennessee, for his teachings about the life of Joseph. I give him credit for these insights.

Chapter 4

1. Reese's name has been changed to protect her privacy.

2. Oswald Chambers, *My Utmost for His Highest*, December 31, accessed March 31, 2014, http://utmost.org/yesterday/.

Chapter 5

1. Hudson Russell Davis, "The Relational Economy: Currency—Part 3," *Crosswalk.com Singles*, accessed March 31, 2014, http://www.crosswalk.com/family/singles/the-relational-economy-currency-part-3.html?p=2.

2. Although this quote has been attributed to both Max Lucado and Maya Angelou, the original source of the quote is unknown.

Chapter 6

1. Laurel Thatcher Ulrich, "Vertuous Women Found: New England Ministerial Literature, 1668-1735," *American Quarterly* 28, no. 1 (Spring 1976): 20.

2. John Piper, "You Will Never Be Thirsty Again" (sermon, June 14, 2009), http://www.desiringgod.org/resource-library/sermons/you-will-never-be-thirsty-again).

Chapter 7

1. Sarah Dornbos, "what I want you to know: being 33 and single," *Rage Against the Minivan* (blog), April 9, 2011, http://www.rageagainsttheminivan.com/2011/04/what-i-want-you-to-know-being-33-and.html.

2. Elayne Boosler, BrainyQuote.com, Xplore Inc, 2014. http://www.brainyquote.com/quotes/quotes/e/elayneboos136073.html, accessed May 5, 2014.

3. Liz Curtis Higgs, "General Session Keynote Address" (speech, Mount Hermon Christian Writers Conference, Felton, CA, March 30, 2012). For more of Higgs's commentary on the book of Ruth, see her book *The Girl's Still Got It: Take a Walk with Ruth and the God Who Rocked Her World* (Colorado Springs, CO: WaterBrook Press, 2012).

4. Brother Lawrence, *The Practice of the Presence of God*, comp. Father Joseph de Beaufort (Rush Springs, OK: RDMc Publishing, 2012), 3rd letter.

Chapter 8

1. Brant Hansen, *Mornings with Brant*, WAY-FM, Nashville, TN, February 11, 2011.

Chapter 9

1. Dornbos, "what I want you to know."

Chapter 10

1. Francis Chan, *Crazy Love: Overwhelmed by a Relentless God*, Kindle ed. (Colorado Springs, CO: David C. Cook, 2008), 59.